FROM THE WINGS

FROM THE WINGS

Amman Memoirs 1947–1951

SIR ALEC KIRKBRIDE

FRANK CASS : LONDON

First Published in 1976 in Great Britain by
FRANK CASS AND COMPANY LIMITED
67 Great Russell Street, London WC1B 3BT, England

and in United States of America by
FRANK CASS AND COMPANY LIMITED
c/o International Scholarly Book Services, Inc.
10300 S. W. Allen Boulevard, Beaverton, Oregon 97005

ISBN 0 7146 3061 6

·Printed in Great Britain by
T. J. Press (Padstow) Ltd., Padstow, Cornwall

Contents

CHAPTER 1

Clearing the Decks

A Chief Secretary of the Government of Palestine, Sir Harry Luke, once remarked to me, in a patronising manner, that the administrative set-up east of the river Jordan was only a temporary expedient. I assumed him to imply that the regime which he represented was more permanent. He was mistaken, because towards the end of 1947, the conclusion of another chapter in the troublous history of Palestine was marked by the announcement of His Majesty's Government of their decision to relinquish, on May 15th of the following year, the mandate over Palestine which they had held since 1920. This renunciation was prompted by the acceptance by the United Nations Organisation of a resolution providing for the partition of Palestine into three states, one Arab, one Jewish and one international. This scheme, which was accepted by the Jews and rejected by the Arabs, was regarded by the British Government as being unworkable. The British authorities were already irked by the fact that their armed forces and the personnel of the Palestine Civil Service were targets for terrorist attacks by both Jews and Arabs and they were not prepared to attempt to implement a scheme which required for its success a degree of co-operation between the two sections of the population which would not be forthcoming. I did not disagree with the British attitude but I did not like the manner in which the policy of withdrawal was carried out.

The news of the intention to withdraw was, at first, received with incredulity by the majority of the Arab peoples and their governments. This reaction was another manifestation of the negative attitude which the Palestinian Arab leaders had adopted towards attempts to solve the country's political problems, from the time of the British occupation onwards, and which had done the Arab cause immense harm. The Arab intransigence would permit no compromise and they insisted on what they regarded as being their rights, with a complete disregard for the consequences of their attitude. One of them had said to Glubb, 'It is better for all to be exterminated than for us to agree to give up a foot of our country.' It had sounded very noble but it had not been very practical.

As always, the Jewish reaction to the announcement was positive and they pressed on with their own preparations for the open warfare which the departure of the British forces from the country would render almost inevitable.

In Jordan, I had no difficulty in convincing King Abdullah and his Ministers that the British Government really meant what they said and were not indulging in the clever political trickery for which they were so undeservedly credited in Levantine minds. The immediate response of the Jordanian authorities was not to prepare for a conflict, but to endeavour to ensure that such a thing did not take place. They were amongst the few Arab leaders who did not underrate their opponents, and the King was the only Arab ruler who had the moral courage to voice his fears about the outcome of an appeal to arms. All that his frankness brought him were accusations of being a traitor to the Arab cause and, ultimately, a violent death.

It was remarkable that the majority of the politicians who held power in Jordan were themselves of Palestinian origin,* yet they evinced a political wisdom which was so woefully absent amongst the influential leaders in their native land. The example and leadership of King Abdullah no doubt had a powerful effect. Soon after he had first established his position in Transjordan in 1921, the King had sought to come to terms with the aspirations of the Jewish people. His motives for so doing were practical. He had appreciated the strength of the forces behind the Zionist movement and he had realised that Jewish enmity could weaken his own chances of achieving his ambition to be accepted by the world as a reigning monarch. The basic solution to the problem which he had always advocated had been a 'Semitic Kingdom' embracing both Palestine and Transjordan, as the eastern part of the mandated territory was then known, in which Arabs and Jews could live as of right and as equals. The scheme included the provision, however, that Jews resident abroad were not to have an automatic right to come to Palestine and immigration controls of some sort would be imposed. It is hardly necessary to add that the King proposed to provide a dynasty to rule the new state.

The idea had won some support from Jewish intellectuals such as Judah Magnes, Martin Buber, Jacob Haas and Haim Kalvaresky, but, once the Jewish Labour Party had won control of the Jewish political institutions in Palestine, the King's policy had lost any small chance of success it might have ever possessed. The majority in the Histadruth, the Jewish Federation of Labour, had always stood out for nothing short of an independent Jewish state. His Majesty's Government had never taken up a position on the subject of the 'Semitic Kingdom', but, on the other hand, they had done nothing to discourage the conception.

King Abdullah had not been the first member of the Hashemite family to discuss with a Jewish leader the possibility of co-operation in Palestine between the two peoples.

* See appendix.

In 1918, his younger brother the Amir, later King Faisal, had received a visit at Abu Lisal, near to Ma'an in southern Jordan, from Dr Haim Weizmann. The outcome of the talks had been a vaguely worded accord, which was actually signed by both parties, but from which nothing practical had emerged because the Amir Faisal had inserted, at the last moment, a rider to the effect that the agreement would be null and void unless the whole of the Arab lands became independent once the war was over. The fact that the meeting took place was, however, an indication that the Arab position was not entirely rigid at that time.

With this background in mind, it is easy to understand why the King made direct contact with the Jewish leaders when it became apparent that the partition scheme would probably be approved by the United Nations Organisation. He was anxious to reinsure his own position in the event of Palestine being split up.

He met Mrs Golda Meyerson, who later changed her name to Meir, and who was head of the Political Department of the Jewish Agency at the time of the meeting. In due course, she became Prime Minister of Israel. Their talk took place at Jisr al-Majami in the house of Mr Avraham Rutenberg, one of the founders of the Palestine Electricity Corporation, whose hydro-electric generating station on the Jordan river stood partly in Jordanian territory. The date was on November 10th 1947. No particular pains were taken up to keep the occasion secret and there was no violent reaction in the other Arab countries when the occurrence became known. The event was not, however, forgotten by the King's enemies.

The King once told me that he had frequently obtained unexpected advantages by following the policy of talking to anybody who was concerned with a problem and of being as charming as was possible in the process. This was evidently the spirit in which he spoke to Mrs Meyerson. He revived the idea of the semitic kingdom but did not persist on that line when he was met with a blank negative in response. He went on to announce his intention of annexing to Transjordan – that part of Palestine allotted to the Arabs under the terms of the partition scheme, but he assured his visitor of his friendship and he promised that Jordan would never attack the Jews. He spoke disparagingly of the other Arab statesmen and described Haj Amin el-Husseini, the ex-Mufti of Jerusalem and the head of the more extreme nationalists, as being their common enemy. Both of them agreed entirely that the internationalisation of Jerusalem was unacceptable. The interview ended on a cordial note and they agreed to meet again after the partition resolution had been passed in New York.

I thought that it was a mistake for the Israelis to be represented by a lady. King Abdullah was very old-fashioned in his outlook and, while he respected the opposite sex, he did not feel that women were the equals of men and disapproved of their playing a political role. He could not be wholly at his ease when talking business to a woman and, in the case in question, notably considered that his dignity would have been better served if the other side had been represented by a man. On the other hand, Mrs Meyerson had had little prior experience in dealing with Arabs and certainly none in negotiating with an Arab potentate. It was a pity that someone like Mr Sharret, speaking the tongue and familiar with the mental processes of the Arabs, did not undertake the mission.

The promised second meeting did not take place until just before the outbreak of hostilities but contact was maintained during the intervening period through third parties. Later on, when rumours became current that the Jordanian Government had decided to join other Arab states in an invasion of Palestine, designed to seize the whole of the country, the King had replied to a query sent to him by Mrs Meyerson with an assurance that his original promise still held good.

Once the Arab leaders realised that the British mandate

really was coming to an end, they authorised the secretariat of the Arab League, which was under the direction of the Egyptian politician Abdel Rahman Azzam, to organise a private army of its own to be paid for from league funds. They accepted that the invasion of Palestine was the next step in the struggle and they planned to create an Arab force for that purpose, for which no one Arab state could be held individually responsible. It would then be possible for that force to move into Palestine before the departure of the British formations. The Arabs appreciated that the departure of the British army on May 15th would leave the Jewish Hagana and Palmach more or less in their battle positions, whereas the regular Arab armies would be on the wrong side of the frontier. It was planned that the Arab League's army should seize and hold points of strategic importance until the regulars arrived.

The new corps was called the Army of Deliverance. It was recruited and trained in military camps in Syria and its commander, the notorious Fawzi al-Kaowkji, was a native of that country, who had acquired a reputation as a successful guerrilla leader during the Arab rebellion in Palestine during the years 1937-39. In point of fact, he had done little to merit the fame which had been created for him by favourable propaganda in the Arab press. At the end of the fighting, he and his men had been virtually surrounded by the British forces in the Jenin district of Samaria, but when an operation designed to destroy him and his guerrillas had been on the point of being put into effect, the High Commissioner of the day, Sir Arthur Wauchope, had issued orders that the rebels were to be permitted to make their way over the frontier into Jordan and on to Iraq, unmolested by the British troops. The reason for this action had been the desire to avoid giving a fillip to the rebellion, which had showed signs of dying down, by the creation of a lot of martyrs. Fawzi had suspected a trap and had refused to move until I had given a personal guarantee of his immunity from attack by Royal Air Force armoured cars when he reached the flat country on his way to Iraq.

Afterwards, Fawzi had showed no gratitude for his escape but had entertained all those who would listen to him with stirring accounts of the way his command had burst their way to freedom through the British lines. The leading elements of the Army of Deliverance crossed from Syria to Palestine in December 1947 and were followed at intervals by the main body and their commander. He was last to arrive and travelled via Amman in February 1948. The move was not welcome to King Abdullah who felt that the newcomers, as servants of the Arab League, were not likely to favour his aspirations with regard to the future of Palestine, but, he did not feel strong enough at that time to voice his opposition nor to place any obstacles in their path.

Having got into position on Palestine soil, Fawzi could not content himself with waiting in the role assigned to him and he embarked on a series of attacks on Jewish settlements which were invariably unsuccessful in spite of his bombastic claims to the contrary. The first objective which he chose was a village of orthodox Jews in the Jordan Valley called Tirat Zvi. He launched his infantry in a charge over open ground, against loopholed buildings, without preliminary artillery bombardment but his forces were repulsed with relatively heavy loss. His wounded casualties were treated at the government hospital in Nablus. The next objective was the settlement of Mishmar ha Emek in the plain of Esdralon. Fawzi brought his guns into action for the first time but they made no impression on the concrete bunkers of the defenders and, eventually, the precious artillery had to be withdrawn in a hurry to avoid capture by Jewish reinforcements sent into action by adjacent settlements.

In fact, Fawzi proved himself in both his campaigns, to be little short of a menace to his own side and his men were to pay dearly during the following months for his omission to provide proper field ambulances and hospitals for his army. He explained afterwards that he had not anticipated having to fight so prolonged a campaign, and he had thought that a few medical officers and their orderlies would meet the needs of the situation.

The troops under his command were of little military value, although many of them had once served in one or other of the regular Arab armies. Indeed, some of his officers and non-commissioned personnel were still active members of the Syrian forces who had been granted indefinite leave of absence from their units. The Syrian Army had also provided the artillery train which consisted of French 75 and 105 millimetre guns carried on hired motor transport.

The next effort of the Army of Deliverance was to deploy its batteries on the Nebi Samwil ridge just to the north-west of Jerusalem and to shell the Jewish quarters of that city with their guns in full view of the British military headquarters. The act was more in the nature of a nuisance than a danger and the intruders withdrew at once when they were threatened with an air strike by Royal Air Force machines.

The arrival on the scene of the Army of Deliverance made the military array in Palestine an absurdity. The Jewish Hagana mobilised and came into the open. The British forces, on the other hand, became unduly preoccupied with the preservation of their own safety and they retired into a series of fortified zones which were the only areas in which the writ of the Palestine Government was unquestioned in its authority. British intervention in the maintenance of law and order outside those zones was limited to cases of extreme urgency as Fawzi's bombardment of Jerusalem.

The Arabs of Palestine started, belatedly, creating paramilitary organisations of their own to which the general name of 'Fighters' was applied.

To confuse the issue still more, these Arab formations were divided between those who took their orders from the political party of the ex-Mufti of Jerusalem and the section controlled by what was sometimes known as the Nashashibi party which was in opposition. Inevitably, there was little co-operation between the two groups of the Fighters.

The existence of so many irregular armies was bound to attract some queer characters who were ready to hire out their services as mercenaries or who hoped to acquire some booty. I noticed two men in Amman who were wearing what appeared to be the uniform of the Turkish General Staff. As the intrusion of two Turkish staff officers without any prior notice from somewhere was highly unlikely, I alerted my Turkish colleague in the diplomatic corps. He interviewed the two 'majors' and discovered that they were not Turks at all but Poles who had learnt a smattering of the Turkish language in Stamboul. The two adventurers, who were taken aback at finding a Turkish diplomat at Amman to unmask them, explained that they wished to fight for the Arab cause on account of their dislike for the Jews. Their services were not used and they disappeared from the scene.

The final complication of the situation in Palestine was provided by the presence of seven infantry companies of the Arab Legion which were employed on the protection of British military installations and paid for by His Majesty's Government. These were formations which had been raised during the war years and had rendered such useful services that they had been kept on until 1948. Their original duties had been varied in the meanwhile and had come to include that of providing a guard for the Iraqi Consulate in Jerusalem.

When raised they had been intended for guard duties only, but in spite of the limitations of their training, they proved, in the event, to be a useful reserve to the four bedouin mechanised regiments which formed the fighting backbone of the Jordanian army.

As part of the army of occupation, the legionaries of the infantry companies were also a target for Jewish terrorist actions and there was an awkward case when an Arab soldier, whose unit had suffered from grenade attacks, shot a Jewish youth who had just thrown an orange at the truck in which he was riding. The Attorney General of Palestine, Gibson, demanded that the man should be arrested and tried by the civil courts, but Glubb, supported by the General Officer Commanding Troops in Palestine, Major General D'Arcy, refused to accept the jurisdiction of the civil administration over personnel of the Arab Legion. It was argued that, in any case, the soldier could not be expected, after what had happened elsewhere, to wait and see whether the missile was harmless before taking steps to protect himself. The military authorities won the bad-tempered wrangle which followed and the offender was removed to Jordan and kept there. No disciplinary action was taken against him.

The various departments of the civil administration were in the process of winding up their affairs. Operating from within the relatively safe refuge of the army security zones, their control over events outside the barbed-wire enclosures diminished as time passed. For a while, I continued my former practice of visiting the High Commissioner for Palestine, General Sir Alan Cunningham, and discussing current affairs with him. The series of visits had been commenced at the time when he had also been High Commissioner for Jordan and I had been his deputy in that country. I found that he and the Chief Secretary, Sir Henry Gurney, were becoming more and more out of touch with reality and were, in a sense, functioning in a vacuum. They lived in their closely guarded safety zones and issued orders which were intended for observance by Jews and Arabs who had, by this time, taken charge of their own affairs and no longer regarded themselves as being bound, either legally or morally, to take any notice of the British authorities. I considered it absurd for the High Commissioner to summon to Government House leaders of both peoples and there solemnly admonish them for not being good. They put pressure on me to compel the Jordanians to behave as though they were satellites of Great Britain. Moreover, their thoughts and mine seemed to travel in different directions. Their aim seemed to be to keep affairs running as though nothing had changed or was going to change. They were on the way out and did not care if the edifice of government was on the point of collapse, but I was to stay on and I was anxious to save something from the wreck.

My visits to Government House entailed my taking risks which did not decrease as time passed and, finally, my wife protested and demanded that they should cease. I had to admit, under her hostile cross-examination, that Cunningham hardly ever took the advice which I tendered and that there was, therefore, little justification for my continuing to endanger my life and that of my driver, in order to give him the benefit of my wisdom.

There was another consideration which prompted my decision to cease going to Jerusalem in spite of my desire to be helpful. When the Hashemite Kingdom of Jordan had become an independent state in 1946, I had ceased to be British Resident responsible to the Colonial Office and I had been appointed Envoy Extraordinary and Minister Plenipotentiary under the Foreign Office, but I had still remained a pensionable District Commissioner in the Palestine Administrative service seconded to the Foreign Service. Both Cunningham and Gurney seemed to find it difficult to accept me as a genuine head of a diplomatic mission and they tended to give me instructions, which they had no right to do and which I had no intention of obeying unless I happened to agree with them. I did not say anything to them on the subject but the message probably got through to them when I ceased to find it convenient to go and call upon them in their lair.

While the affairs of Palestine continued to slide gradually into a state of chaos, the Foreign Office took a little more interest in Jordan. In the spring of 1948, the Prime Minister, Tewfiq abul Huda, and Glubb were invited to go to London, ostensibly to agree on the text of some unimportant amendment to the Anglo-Jordanian Treaty of Friendship, but the real and undeclared item of importance on the agenda was to discuss the future intentions of the Jordanian Government with regard to Palestine.

The visitors told the Secretary of State, Mr Ernest Bevin, that Transjordan proposed to occupy peacefully, at the end of the Mandate, those parts of Palestine which had been allocated to the Arabs in the scheme of partition approved by the United Nations. They told me that Mr Bevin reacted to the statement by saying that that course of action seemed to be a sensible thing to do. Some Arab writers, including Fadhil el-Jamali of Iraq, attributed to Mr Bevin other openly hostile remarks about the Jews, but I am sure that the account given to me by Tewfiq and Glubb was accurate.

I was too preoccupied with urgent problems in Amman to be able to spare the time to go to London for this meeting, but I was consulted telegraphically, when the conference was convened, about the real intentions of the King and his Ministers. I advised the Secretary of State that I was convinced that the Jordanians were honest in their plan to restrict their occupation in Palestine to the Arab zone and to avoid a clash between the Arab Legion and the Jewish forces. I still think that my conclusion was right, but it should have been evident to all of us concerned, having regard to the fighting which was already taking place in Palestine, that the chances of a peaceful occupation being effected by the Arab Legion were so small as to be negligible. Not long after expressing this opinion, I reached the conclusion that war between the Arabs and the Jews was inevitable and that, when it came, it would be impossible for the Jordanians to stand aloof from the conflict. Public sentiment throughout the Arab world would be more powerful than the good intentions and promises expressed to Mrs Meyerson.

I conveyed this pessimistic view to the Foreign Office and all and sundry who came to see me at Amman. The last category included Mr Ortiguez, a member of the Palestine Conciliation Commission appointed to reconcile the irreconcilable. I told him that I had never seen two peoples more determined to fight each other. He left me in a more depressed state of mind than that in which he arrived.

Glubb and the Jordanian Ministers were not long in arriving at the same conclusion as myself and they began, as unobtrusively as was possible, to plan for a fight which they did not want. One of the principal difficulties with which they had to contend was the fact that the Jordanian Government, and in particular the Arab Legion, lived in a hand-to-mouth dependence on Great Britain for financial aid, arms and ammunition. They had no reserves and no alternative sources from which money and equipment could be found. It was also evident that the Ministers did not appreciate the implications of going to war because the Prime Minister staggered Glubb, when the latter asked for a supplementary budget, by telling him that the Arab Legion would have to fight on its normal financial allocation. Other problems arose from the many tactical and strategic questions which had to be decided by persons who had had no previous experience in such matters.

The decease of the Palestine Civil Service entailed a change in my own status and I was faced with the alternative of a transfer to another post of similar seniority elsewhere in the Colonial Service or retirement on my colonial pension and temporary employment in Jordan by the Foreign Office for an indefinite period. It was unlikely that a new post in the Colonial Service would be in an Arab country and, in any case, I had never served in a Crown Colony and did not want to start afresh in one. So I elected to stay where I was. No pressure was brought to bear on me, either one way or the other, but I had reason to suppose that the powers that be would be pleased if I stayed on in Amman.

CHAPTER 2

On The Brink

The only regular Arab troops to be left in Palestine during
the last days of the mandate were to be the infantry companies of the Arab Legion and it was a foregone conclusion that they would be withdrawn before the evacuation
of the British Forces. Their departure would leave the
Hagana in a more favourable position vis-à-vis the Arab
armies which could not move in over the frontier before
May 15th. It was, therefore, important that once they
could advance, the Arabs should get into position with
as little delay as was possible.

The Arab League had elaborated an overall plan of
operations and this provided that the main fighting force
of the Arab Legion should be established in a matter
of hours after the commencement of the moves on the
high ridge which lay between Ramallah and Jerusalem,
and so dominate the centre of Palestine in any direction.
There were two macadamised roads by which the Arab
Legion could march into that position from its assembly
points in the Jordan Valley. The shorter route, which
had a better surface than the alternative was that from
the Allenby Bridge through Jericho and the outskirts of
Jerusalem where it passed within rifle range of the Jewish
Quarter of the Old City and could not, therefore, be used
freely by Arab convoys.

The other way was the alignment passing up the Wadi Fara to Nablus and thence down the north-south main road to Ramallah. The use of the latter route would entail a serious loss of time for heavily ladened vehicles and armour, to say nothing of the extra expenditure on fuel. Local informants stated, however, and a reconnaissance confirmed that there was a rough track, which ran up a spur of the mountain to the west of Jericho, and which could, at a pinch, be made passable for the use of wheeled traffic during the dry season of the year. It was not to be expected that the work of improvement which could be done in the few weeks which remained for preparations, could produce a good enough surface of a permanent nature but it was hoped that the track would not be needed any more after the initial advance had been made by a route not known to the enemy.

The track in question was an ancient ridgeway and may well have been the one used by the Israelites under the leadership of Joshua when they moved up into the highlands, after seizing Jericho, to capture the town of Ai and go on to their first conquest of Palestine about the year 1200 BC. It was an interesting repetition of history, with the role of the Israelis reversed in that they were now to be the invaded instead of being the invaders.

At that stage of the withdrawal, the British departmental personnel of the Palestine Civil Service had little idea of what their Arab and Jewish colleagues were doing and the latter were each working for whatever they deemed to be in the best interests of their respective aides. In such circumstances, it was a simple matter for the Trans-jordanian authorities to arrange with the Arabs who staffed the Jericho division of the Department of Public Works to undertake the task of making the track in question passable. The Arab Legion provided the necessary funds to pay the labourers, six thousand pounds, and lent the workmen a number of tools.

The work was completed within the time available and was ready to be used during the first advance of the

Jordanian troops. The most remarkable thing about the affair was that the secret, which was known to almost every Arab in the sub-district, did not appear to have reached the Jewish Intelligence officers who were, as a rule, very well informed. On the British side, only a handful of the officials serving in Jordan were in the know. I was one of these but I did not consider it my business to carry tales to anyone, either locally or in London.

When told the story, years afterwards, a friend of mine raised two queries. He asked how it was possible for so large a payment to be concealed in the accounts of the Arab Legion without its purpose being evident, and secondly, why the item was not spotted in the course of the British control over the expenditure of the Jordanian government? Briefly, the answers were that the provision for contingencies in so large a budget as that of the Arab Legion, or rather, the Ministry of Defence, could cover a multitude of sins; secondly, that after Transjordan became independent in 1946, all financial supervision by the British Government ceased and the Jordanian Government was free to spend as it liked the subsidy which was received under the terms of the treaty. The money in question was ear-marked to meet the cost of the Arab Legion.

The almost complete loss of control over events by the Palestine administration during the last few months of its existence was illustrated also by the ludicrous conditions which prevailed at the Allenby Bridge where the principal road between Amman and Jerusalem crossed over the Jordan river. The Palestine Police and Customs services kept up a show of activity at their posts on the bridge regardless of the fact that, about a hundred and fifty yards upstream, and in full view of those who were supposed to be controlling the frontier, some local fishermen provided an unauthorised ferry service over the water for the use of travellers who were without travel documents or who had some other reason for wishing to avoid going through the normal formalities. The charge made for the use of the ferry was only half a pound per head.

Still further to the north and round a bend in the river, there was yet another ferry for which the minimum charge was a pound. It was explained to those interested, that the visible ferry was there to serve the convenience of relatively innocent travellers, while the other crossing, which was round the bend, was for the use of smugglers, armed rebels, escaped convicts and the like.

One Sunday morning, when I was beating through the bushes for black partridge near to the eastern end of the expensive ferry, I came face to face with a young Arab who was dressed in a khaki uniform of sorts but was not carrying arms. He looked startled when he saw me, probably because I was carrying a gun and he was not. I greeted him politely and asked him where he was coming from. In reply, he first enquired whether I was an official of the local government and, when I assured him, quite truthfully, that I was nothing to do with government at Amman, he admitted that he was deserting from the Army of Deliverance. He added the remark that life was becoming too dangerous for comfort 'over there'. Apparently, he had sold his rifle and ammunition to pay himself the arrears of salary which were due to him.

One of the problems of the British liquidation which caused considerable apprehension was the disbanding of the Transjordan Frontier Force. In spite of its name, it had no connection with the Jordanian Government although King Abdullah happened to be its honorary Colonel-in-Chief. Its camps were situated in Jordan, and in Palestine and its members included a large proportion of Palestinian Arabs most of whom were deeply involved emotionally in the future fate of their country. There were also many men whose length of service did not qualify them for pensions and who would, therefore, have little to lose by deserting with their arms and enlisting in one of the various Arab fighting forces of a less regular character which were in the market to hire the services of trained men. In spite of the temptations, there were few deserters when the time came, owing largely to the personal influence of the commanding officer, Colonel (later General) J. Hackett. The break took place in an orderly manner and without leaving any ill feeling.

There was slight cloud over the final parade which King Abdullah was not invited to attend, although it took place in one of the camps in Jordanian territory. Instead, the salute was taken by the High Commissioner for Palestine, Sir Alan Cunningham. The King did not protest at this breach of protocol but he had his own back by refusing to sanction a series of awards of Jordanian honours recommended by Hackett for some of the outgoing Arab officers and men. The proposed local decorations were replaced by British awards which I had the honour of presenting to the recipients at my legation during the months to come. Amidst all the turmoil, I had to write a formal despatch to the Foreign Office to report the issue of each M.B.E.

As far as preparations on the West Bank were concerned, the army commanders and the civil authorities showed remarkably little interest in what might happen after their departure. The United Nations Organisation appointed a commission to arrange for the maintenance of essential services during and after the British evacuation, but its members achieved nothing in the face of the non-co-operative stand of the authorities which made any orderly transfer of power impossible. Subsequent criticism for this state of affairs was met with the excuse that the Palestine administration could not abdicate its authority before the legal termination of the mandate. This also was unconvincing to those like myself who saw how far the responsible quarters abdicated their duties when it suited them to do so.

There was one exception made to this studied lack of foresight. It was in favour of the Palestine Archeological Museum at Jerusalem, on the grounds that this beautiful building and its remarkable collection of antiquities were

of international interest. The institution had not been
created with funds of the Palestine Government but had
been built and endowed with money provided by the
Rockefeller Foundation of the United States of America,
so that there was special justification for taking exceptional
steps to assure it an independent status. Legislation was
enacted transferring its ownership and future management
to a board of trustees of which the representative of His
Majesty's Government in Jordan would be an ex-officio
member. The other trustees were to be the nominees
of certain learned institutions, including the Hebrew
University in Jerusalem, and a representative of the
Jordan Government. The inclusion of a Jewish member
was an interesting piece of optimism but the University's
representative, Mr Sukenik, was never able to attend a
meeting. While the legal framework of the change was
created, nothing was done to convene the board before
May 15th.

The Palestinian Arab leaders tried desperately to prepare themselves for the coming storm, once they were
convinced, albeit belatedly, that a storm was in the offing.
Most of their endeavours were in pursuit of matters which
could only be of limited military value. One of their objec-
tives, for instance, was the supply and ordinance depot
of the British forces at Sarafand. The place was not capable of being defended individually and could only be
of use to those who were in control of the surrounding
countryside. It was next door to Tel Aviv and likely, therefore, to be in the Jewish sector when the fighting
commenced.

I was only directly affected by this futile sort of scheme
when the Palestinians sought, at almost the last moment,
to gain possession of the section of the narrow gauge
Hejaz Railway which lay in Palestinian territory between
Acre, Haifa and Semakh. That section of the railway ran
through one of the most thickly populated areas of Jewish
owned real estate and it was clear that it could only be
of use to the Arabs, strategically or otherwise, if and

when the Jewish forces were defeated. Nevertheless, King Abdullah and Tewfiq abul Huda were induced to pester me to persuade the British Government, who were the custodians of the line, to transfer the railway to the Arabs before the day of evacuation. The request was based on the argument that the line was a Moslem Pious Foundation, a point which was debatable, and that, as such, it should be administered by the Moslem world. Nobody on the British side was interested in the matter of the Hejaz Railway and it was left, together with the other assets of the state, for the Arabs and the Jews to fight over.

Apart from those of them who enlisted in one of the para-military organisations which were set up, many of the Arabs armed themselves with an astounding selection of more or less serviceable lethal weapons, though few of them had any prior experience in the use of arms. The net result of all these preparations for war was not reassuring and, when the Arab League sent a staff officer of the Iraqi Army on a clandestine inspection of the defensive arrangements made in the principal Arab towns, he was appalled. He called on King Abdullah on his way back to Cairo and expressed the opinion that none of the Arab centres of population were capable of standing up to a serious attack. Events were to prove him right.

This adverse report did not discourage the Iraqi Government from making their contribution to the array of Arab armies which were preparing to invade Palestine. An Iraqi Expeditionary Force of approximately brigade strength, with some aircraft, moved to Mafrak in northern Jordan and prepared to take over the northern sector of the front in the Jordan Valley between the Dead Sea and the Sea of Galilee. The force included a Lieutenant Colonel Abdel Kerim Qassem of whom a lot more was to be heard. He was one of the future military dictators who served on the Arab side in the coming war. The commander of the Iraqi contingent paid a formal call on King Abdullah and the latter was subsequently entertained by the Iraqis at Mafrak.

His Majesty's Government were not consulted by the Jordanians about the movement of the force; I reported the facts to London, and nothing was said by them on the subject.

The other Iraqi ranks were not, on the whole, a desirable lot and their morals, or rather lack of morals, made them unpopular with the local population. Few of the men were permitted to visit Amman or the other towns in Jordan.

Whilst all these preparations were in train, two last ditch attempts were made to keep Jordan from becoming involved in the threatening conflict. They were, firstly, an enquiry by King Abdullah, through an emissary, as to whether the Jewish leaders would be prepared to cede to him some of the land allotted to them in the partition scheme, so as to provide him with an excuse for pressing the Arab world to accept the division of Palestine. He was told that no such concession was possible and that the acceptance of the boundaries described in the plan approved by the United Nations Organisation was subject to the partition scheme being implemented as a whole, and in a peaceful fashion. If the Arabs went to war, the Jews would retain anything that they could win.

Even before the first move was made by the King, the Jewish leaders had decided to make direct contact with him once again. A meeting was arranged for May 18th but this time, the King was more anxious to keep the occasion secret and he declined to go to Jisr Majami. News of the previous meeting was widely known and the King could not afford to create, at a time of crisis, further suspicion in the Arab world about his motives and intentions. The upshot was a decision that Mrs Meyerson and her party should go to Amman in disguise and meet the King there in a private house. Mrs Meyerson, who was dressed as an Arab lady, made the journey accompanied by a Mr Ezra Dannin who spoke Arabic well enough to pass as a native. They were picked up by a palace car at the Jisr Majami power house after they took extraordinary precautions in Palestine to conceal their ultimate destination.

The meeting took place in a cordial atmosphere although Mrs Meyerson afterwards described the King as having been depressed and nervous. When reminded of his earlier promise not to attack the Jews, the King replied that the position had changed. The Jewish representatives took this remark to mean that the directives of His Majesty's Government had changed. They were mistaken in this assumption, no advice had been given to the King on either occasion; in fact, the British Government had assumed an attitude of detachment. The King revived, once again, the proposal to form a joint Judeo-Arab kingdom and asked for more patience on the part of the Jews. The response to his gambit was entirely negative and it was evident that neither side had anything significant to offer the other. Finally, the visitors warned the King to take more precautions when receiving Arab callers because there were many current reports of plots against his life. The whole exercise proved to have been futile and might easily have been disastrous because the driver of the car lost his nerve on the return journey and put his passengers down in the Jordan Valley, a few miles short of their destination, and left them to complete the trip on foot.

The next caller of note at Amman was Abder Rahman Azzam who probably came there with the express intention of making sure that the Jordanian authorities did not fail to play the part assigned to them in the plan drawn up by the Arab League. He had several talks with Glubb and, surprisingly enough, offered him the appointment by the League to the post of Commander-in-Chief of all the Arab forces in the field. Both Glubb and I were convinced that the offer was made in bad faith and that none of the other Arab governments would be prepared to permit their troops to be placed under the orders of a British officer, even if he was technically a servant of the Jordanian Government. We suspected that the hidden idea behind the proposal was to provide a ready-made scapegoat for any future failures. Anyway, the suggestion was rejected with something approaching derision.

Azzam took the initiative in arranging to meet the High Commissioner and the Chief Secretary, Gurney, at Jericho. My knowledge of what transpired between them was limited to what Azzam told me afterwards. He said that his intention had been to make certain arrangements which would have been to the benefit of the Arabs after the evacuation but that he had achieved nothing. The others had been unsympathetic and had infuriated him by trying to give him orders as to what was or was not to be done by the Arab armies after the 15th of the month. His voice shook with anger as he told me about the interview. My own opinion, which I did not express, was that the two British officials had not been in a position to do anything for anybody, even had they wished to be helpful.

After the Jericho fiasco, Azzam expressed the wish to meet me on neutral ground. His idea of a neutral place proved to be the private residence of a mutual Arab acquaintance, Ismail Bilbeīsī, where we met on May 15th. After an exchange of insincere compliments, he told me about the abortive meeting at Jericho. He next asked me for an assurance that the British forces from Palestine, who were congregated in the north of Sinai, would not cut off the retreat of the Egyptian army formations if the latter advanced into Palestine. I felt able to reply that, in my view, any such move by our forces would be highly unlikely. He pressed me for a more categorical promise but he declined to take advantage of my offer to refer the matter to the Foreign Office.

After some more havering, he stood up, struck a pose, and said, dramatically: 'It is my duty to announce to you the intention of the Arab armies to march into Pales-·tine tomorrow at midnight!' I retorted that the news did not surprise me. He went on to enumerate the approximate strengths of the various Arab armies available for the influx and, when I asked him for his estimate of the size of the Jewish forces, waved his hands and said: 'It does not matter how many there are. We will sweep them into the sea!' He became quite peevish when I pointed out that, when one was considering a military problem, it was normal to take into account the courses which were open to the enemy as well as those open to one's self. It seemed to me that he was missing out the first part of the exercise. He countered by asking for my estimate of the Jewish strength, but he dismissed as absurd my reply that common report placed it at about eighty thousand people. I put an end to the argument by remarking that it was difficult to talk sensibly if he, while admitting that he did not know the answer, refused to believe what I said to him. We parted on terms which were fairly correct but rather frigid. I never met him again.

I suppose that there was some purpose behind his desire to meet me but it was not apparent. Like the other Arab leaders, he affected in public to be utterly confident about the outcome of the pending conflict but, in reality, he seemed to be suffering from acute anxiety. His host mentioned to me that Azzam had not slept the night before.

The only positive result of Azzam's visit to Amman was the payment to the Jordanian Government of a sum of £250,000 from the funds of the Arab League ear-marked to meet the cost of the war. He described the payment at the time, as a first instalment of an amount of £3,000,000 which was to be issued to Jordan from that source, but in the event the promise was not kept.

Both Glubb and I sensed that Azzam shared the hostility which the Egyptian authorities showed towards King Abdullah and his followers. Azzam was entirely unhelpful in the scandalous case when the Egyptian army seized a shipload of ammunition at Suez which was consigned by the British ordinance depot to the Arab Legion. This high-handed action was all the more reprehensible because the consignment in question proved to be the last opportunity for the Legion to replenish its stocks before the general embargo on the issue of supplies and money was imposed by Great Britain with regard to all the belligerents. The only explanation offered by the Egyptian Government for stealing this ammunition was that they were in urgent need of it themselves. Their needs could not have been greater than those of the Arab Legion, particularly as regards shell for twenty-five pounder guns which made up the bulk of the consignment. Azzam declined to intervene in the matter and the Egyptians refused to return the stores or to refund their value to the Jordanian Government.

One of the final phases of the clearing of the decks for action was the return to Jordanian territory of the seven infantry companies of the Arab Legion which were serving in Palestine under the orders of the British Commander-in-Chief. Some of these men were unduly delayed by the British command so that one of the companies could only beat the deadline by which time it had to leave, by moving with its late employers into Sinai and making its way home through Aqaba. The Egyptian authorities were deeply offended by having Jordanian troops brought into their country although they expected to be accorded freedom of movement in Jordan for their own men.

The last few months before the end of the mandate marked a period of unhappiness for me and I experienced a feeling of helpless horror in much the same way as a bystander watching an impending motor accident knows he can do nothing to prevent it. Some of the Jordanians and most of my colleagues of the diplomatic corps, were convinced that some deep laid plan lay behind the otherwise, to them, inexplicable behaviour of the British Government. By and large, the Arabs believed that the apparent lack of policy concealed a plot on the part of His Majesty's Government to take their revenge on the Palestine Arabs for all that the latter had done in the past to thwart the mandatory power. It is probable that most of the Jewish community thought that the British hoped for an Arab victory which would compel the Jews to beg for Great Britain to resume the position of ruler over Palestine. From what I saw during that period, I was convinced that they were all mistaken in their assessments of the British attitude. I believe that the long history of rebellion and terrorism in Palestine had exhausted the patience and disillusioned the British Ministers to such a point that their one desire was to divest themselves of all future responsibility for what might happen in that troublesome country. The 'could not care less' attitude of many of the British officials who were packing up in Palestine, which I found so irritating, was probably a reflection of the attitude of the people in London.

The few instructions which were sent by the Foreign Office for my guidance were generally negative, such as the telegram stating, in categorical terms, that events west of the river Jordan were to be of no direct concern to my legation. I could report but I was not to interfere.

Personally, I desired fervently that there should be no fighting at all but, as the time drew on and the situation deteriorated, I began to experience the perverse desire for the worst to happen, which comes after a long period of suspense. In other words, if there was to be a war, let us have it and get it over. I hoped that the hostilities would be stopped by international intervention before too much damage was suffered by either protagonist, and that it would be possible to patch up some sort of settlement of their quarrel. I confess that I had no very clear ideas of the lines on which such a settlement could follow.

If the outlook from Amman was grim, it was not as dismal as that which faced Dick Beaumont who was to be stationed at Jerusalem as a Consul General accredited to no one. His office was to be set up in the building standing near to the Damascus Gate, which had been the home of the Secretariat of the Palestine Government in which I had worked many years before, from 1924 to 1927. The staff were to include a guard of ex-soldiers and retired policemen who were recruited specially for the role. The guards were to be armed but it was not intended that they should attempt to resist a hostile army; it was hoped that they would be able to protect the consulate from being looted by a mob or thieves during the period of confusion which was anticipated. In the event, neither of the belligerents permitted any disorder to occur from civilian elements and the guards were not really necessary.

The consular area covering the city of Jerusalem was excluded from the jurisdiction of the British Legation at Amman and later Tel Aviv, in order to preserve the fiction that the city was an internationalised enclave in accordance with the terms of a resolution of the United Nations Organisation. It was a point about which the Foreign Office showed considerable concern although, in practice, the consular work in Jerusalem could have been carried quite easily by the two legations without, in my view, compromising the principle of internationalisation.

Special reference should, perhaps, be made to the detachment of the Royal Air Force which remained at Amman after the evacuation of the British Forces from Palestine. The station had been established there since 1921 and the length of time during which the Royal Air Force had followed an unobtrusive policy of non-interference in the internal affairs of the country, coupled with the willing rendering of help whenever that was needed, had resulted in its occupants being accepted by the majority of the Jordanians as part of the background and not being regarded as members of a foreign army of occupation.

When the mandate terminated over Jordan in 1946, neither party to the Anglo-Jordanian Treaty raised the question of the air force being withdrawn from the country. The retention of the station at Amman was, essentially, a flag flying exercise. The personnel and their aircraft did not constitute a fighting unit and Amman was no longer on an air route which was of strategic or tactical value to Great Britain.

CHAPTER 3

The First Round

At a few minutes before the hour of midnight on May 14–15th, 1948, King Abdullah and members of his personal staff stood at the eastern end of the Allenby Bridge across the river Jordan waiting for the mandate to expire officially. They need not have waited because the British personnel had already gone. At twelve o'clock precisely the King drew his revolver, fired a symbolical shot into the air and shouted the word, 'forward'. The long column of Jordanian troops which stretched down the road behind the bridge, already had the engines of their cars ticking over and, as they moved off at the word of command, the hum of their motors rose to a roar. They passed through Jericho and went up the ridgeway which had been prepared for them and, when daylight came, the first regiment was in position on the Ramallah ridge which was their objective in the Judean highlands. Other units moved up the Wadi Fara into the heart of the Samaria district.

The number ·of front line troops of the Arab Legion then amounted to about four thousand five hundred men who made up four bedouin mechanised regiments, seven infantry companies recruited from townsmen and two four-gunned batteries of twenty-five pounder artillery. The infantry companies were later reorganised on a regimental basis. There were no combatant aircraft in the Legion but the Iraqi Air Force at Mafrak had two flights of obsolete Gladiator fighters and a flight of Anson light bombers which were supposed to be available for co-operation with the Jordanian forces. In practice, however the latter fought virtually without air cover.

Many of the recruits newly enlisted in the bedouin regiments were nationals of Saudi Arabia and came from the warlike tribes of the Nejd whose men had enabled King Abdel Aziz ibn Saud to conquer the best part of the Arabian Peninsula. These men might fairly be described as professional soldiers in the sense that they regarded fighting as the most honourable means by which to earn a living. Their forefathers would have fought and raided their neighbours but, now that the invention of the internal combustion engine had brought law and order to the desert, they had joined in the nearest war available. As a rule, they had no clear political views about what was happening in Palestine when they presented themselves for engagement but many of them, doubtlessly, acquired some ideas on the subject afterwards.

The realisation of the inadequacy of their army's manpower was largely responsible for the decision of the Jordanian command to avoid, as long as it was possible to do so, becoming involved in the fighting in Jerusalem where a rabbit warren of narrow lanes and bazaars would have made the operations too costly in casualties. The lesser consideration that the city had not been allotted to the Arabs under the partition scheme but had been earmarked for internationalisation, no doubt carried some weight in their counsels. In principle, therefore, the defence of the Arab quarters of Jerusalem was left to the irregular formations at the outset.

In the north of the country, the Iraqi detachment moved across the Jordan river at Jisr al-Majami and took up positions in the mountains round Nablus. Shortly after their advance, the Iraqi commander issued a communiqué proudly announcing to the world that his troops had captured an important Jewish power station on the river Jordan. In point of fact, all that they had done was to take over from the Jordanian police the Palestine Electricity Corporation's hydro-electric generating plant which had been voluntarily evacuated by its Jewish staff before the 15th of the month. Some weeks before that date, I had been instructed by the Foreign Office to make representations to the Jordanian authorities about the wisdom of preserving this valuable economic asset intact. I had pointed out that the Jordanians were not likely to accept my intervention on behalf of the property of a local Jewish firm which was registered in Palestine. The people in London thereupon dropped the question.

Further to the north, the Lebanese and Syrian armies made what were hardly more than demonstrations in force along their frontiers with Palestine. The Syrians managed to get as far as the abandoned camp of the Transjordan Frontier Force near to Semakh, on the shore of the Sea of Galilee, and also declared it to be captured.

Elsewhere, the Army of Deliverance took up position in Samaria, between the zones held by the Iraqi Army and the Arab Legion. The Egyptians who put the largest Arab contingent into the field, marched up from Sinai occupying the town of Gaza and stretching their occupation as far to the north as Bethlehem by May 22nd.

All these moves were part of an overall plan of campaign drawn up by the Arab allies in Cairo, but, unfortunately for them, they were almost the only matters on which there was real co-operation among the invaders. It was typical of this lamentable lack of co-operation that rival Jordanian and Egyptian military governors should be appointed to the towns of Hebron and Bethlehem. The two competing governments also opened post offices in which their postage stamps overprinted 'Palestine' were sold. This competition gave the local inhabitants wonderful opportunities to indulge in the game of playing one side against the other.

On the next day after the initial Arab move over the

frontier, the first diplomatic reaction came in the form of a visit to Amman of the Belgian Consul General in Jerusalem, who delivered a formal protest on behalf of the Security Council of the United Nations Organisation against the invasion of Palestine territory by the Arab Legion. Similar futile gestures were made simultaneously in the capitals of the other Arab states which had sent troops into the battle. The Jordanian Minister of Foreign Affairs gave the visitor a cup of coffee and a cigarette and sent him on his way without a formal answer.

The first phase of the war in Palestine developed into a desperate struggle between the Israeli forces and the defenders of the central front for the possession of the city of Jerusalem. It soon became evident that the latter, whose inexperienced ranks had, by this time, been stiffened by discharged personnel of the Transjordan Frontier Force and a group of deserters from the disbanded British section of the Palestine Police, were no match for their opponents. The Arabs did not lack courage or devotion to their cause but they suffered from the evils of a divided command and they were not trained to fight as organised units. Had it not been for the physical obstacle afforded by the sixteenth-century stone ramparts which enclosed the Old City, the Arab positions would probably have been overrun in the first twenty-four hours. I doubt whether their builder, the Turkish Sultan Sulayman the Magnificent, ever imagined that the defensive value of his wall would endure for as long as four hundred years.

Frantic appeals for help from the inhabitants of the city deluged the King and his Ministers and, in the end, Glubb, who had stood out for the agreed policy of non-involvement as long as he could, received orders to go to the rescue in such peremptory terms that they could only be disobeyed at the cost of causing a breach of irreparable gravity between him and the King. The Arab Legion moved one company of about a hundred men into Jerusalem on May 18th and that token force, which was soon followed by further reinforcements, just tipped the scales enough to prevent an Arab collapse there and then.

Although events moved too rapidly for any official representations to be made on instructions from the Foreign Office (if any were ever intended) I spoke privately to the Prime Minister about the probable repercussions of a departure from the original plan to confine the Jordanian occupation to the Arab area of partition. The force of public opinion, however on the subject of Jerusalem, the third most holy shrine of Islam, was too intense for help against the Israeli offensive to be withheld, whatever the consequences of intervention. One must also remember the important consideration to King Abdullah personally of the presence of the tomb of his father King Hussein ibn Ali of the Hejaz, at one of the gates of the Haram es Sherif in Jerusalem. When the old King had been lying on his death bed in the palace at Amman, he had said that because he had once been the guardian of the most holy places of Islam, he wanted his body to rest in another such place.

The front line in Jerusalem was, eventually, more or less stabilised with the Old City and the eastern and northern quarters left in the hands of the Arabs. The building housing the British Consulate General remained in the Arab sector, but only just; the firing line ran along the opposite side of the road from where the office stood and the place was, therefore, exposed entirely to the fire of the Israeli troops whose positions in the French hospice of Notre Dame de France overlooked the locality. One of the British consular guards was killed by a stray bullet and had to be buried temporarily in the garden. The occupants of the building were in a most unpleasant predicament; they were virtually prisoners, short of supplies, unable to sleep through the din of the battle at their gates and they had nothing to do. It was not surprising that at one stage they asked the local commander of the Arab Legion to take his war elsewhere.

The Jewish quarter in the Old City fell during the

fighting prior to the first truce and some fifteen hundred Jewish prisoners were taken by the Arabs. They were well treated by the Arab Legion and only fighting men and others of military age were sent to the internment camp which was set up for them at Mafraq on the edge of the desert. The rest of the captives were delivered across the lines into Israeli territory.

One of the few pleasing developments during this unfortunate time was the respect which the Jordanian and Israeli soldiers showed for each other; a feeling which seemed to be entirely absent in the relationship between the Israelis and the other Arab forces. In one instance, when some lorry loads of prisoners were being driven through the streets of Amman on their way to Mafraq, the Legionary guards, on their own initiative, gave Arab headdresses to those in their charge to protect them from insult, or worse, at the hands of the Palestinian refugees who already thronged the town. One or two of the internees were British subjects and by sending my First Secretary, Christopher Pirie-Gordon, to see to their welfare, I was able to satisfy myself that all of them were being treated humanely. It should be recorded that the treatment meted out to the members of the Arab Legion who fell into the hands of the Israelis was equally satisfactory, although the same cannot be said about the Arab civilians who were taken into custody by the enemy.

The Consulate General of France in Jerusalem was in a similarily exposed position to that of Beaumont's quarters, with the difference that it was just behind the Israeli lines and exposed to fire from the Arab positions. After a French army liaison officer had been wounded by another stray bullet, the Foreign Office apparently forgot about their earlier orders to the effect that events in Palestine were no concern of mine and they directed me to get the Jordanian Government to stop the firing on the French Consulate. They must have intended in the first place, that events west of the river were not, my business unless the Foreign Office made them so. In the case in question, the answer was that the Arabs whose missiles worried the French were firing at Israeli troops positioned near to the Consulate and were, in any case, men of the Fighters and, as such, not under the control of the Jordanian authorities. I forebore making the obvious suggestion that the best way to ensure the immunity of the Frenchmen was for the Israelis to move away from their vicinity.

As I had feared, the intervention of the Arab Legion in Jerusalem brought trouble from His Majesty's Government, who, in response to the terms of a resolution adopted by the United Nations Organisation, suspended the issue to Jordan of all financial aid and military supplies. This action placed the country in a parlous situation because, as I have said already, it had no resources of money and ammunition and depended for current supplies of both on aid from Great Britain. We got a very bad press and the King and his Ministers were both furious and alarmed. The former remarked to me that, 'allies who let one become involved in a war and then cut off our essential supplies are not very desirable friends'.

My explanation that the British Government was acting under directions from the United Nations and that, in any case, the proposal which Mr Bevin had not objected to had been to occupy the Arab part of Palestine under the partition scheme, which did not include Jerusalem—failed to appease the Jordanians. What seemed to rankle most was the fact that no word or warning about possible consequences had been given when they had declared their intentions to the Secretary of State.

The penal embargo on money and supplies was bad enough but, worse was to follow. The staff work of the Arab Legion and the command of the mechanised regiments depended on British officers and I received orders that all such officers who were seconded to the Legion by the War Office, were to cease playing active roles in the military operations in Palestine and were to be withdrawn to the east of of the River Jordan within a specified period of time. This was a severe blow but the terms of the instruction appeared to indicate that there was no use appealing against the ruling, which imposed a heavy administrative handicap on the Legion. The most serious aspect of the matter was the harm done to the morale of the men who would see their officers being taken away from their units in the middle of a battle and the effect of the ban on the Jordanian Ministers. I took steps which enabled me to report that all the personnel concerned were back in Jordan before the deadline set by the Foreign Office, but I was not sure that they stayed there for long.

The British Officers attached to the Arab Legion were of two categories, those seconded from the British armed services, who were in the majority, and the so-called contract officers, who were technically employees of the Jordanian Government. In the sense that he was retired from the British army, Glubb belonged to the second category, but his position was special. When he had been appointed by the Jordanian Government in 1930, as second in command of the Legion, his candidature for the post had been put forward by His Majesty's Government and, when he had taken over the command of the force in 1939, his promotion had been given the official blessing of the British Government. Moreover, in order to give him a pensionable status, he had been appointed to a permanent post on the cadre of the Palestine Police, on the understanding, in fact, that his services would not be used in Palestine.

With two exceptions, the other contract officers were appointed by the local government on recommendations by Glubb and without reference to the British. The two exceptions were Broadhurst, the officer i/c Administration, who served with the Palestine Police before going to Jordan, and Lash, the divisional commander, who was not pensionable in Palestine but whose engagement had been agreed by the Residency.

A subsequent order from London was even more pre-

posterous than those already mentioned. I was told to
warn Glubb and those under his command who were
serving on contracts, that they might be liable to prosecu-
tion in the English Courts under the terms of the Foreign
Enlistment Act for being in the service of a foreign power
engaged in war, without the cognizance of His Majesty's
Government. Glubb, who was livid with anger, wrote back
to me to say, that after selecting him in 1939 to command
the Arab Legion, His Majesty's Government must be
suffering from a grievous loss of memory, to write as
they did. The Foreign Office did not take the matter any
further at that time but more was to be heard later.

In a way, the position was mitigated by the existence
of a secret stock of ammunition for artillery and small
arms which were held in the stores of the Royal Air Force
camp at Amman. Authority for the issue of that material
to the Arab Legion could only be given by the Air Ministry
and, as far as I could understand the matter, such permission would only be given if and when the Israeli forces
invaded Jordanian territory and so brought into play the
protective clauses of the Anglo-Jordanian Treaty. I did
not tell the Jordanians about the presence of these stores
so as to avoid the incessant pleas for their release with
which I would otherwise have been pestered.

At this time, I found myself to be suffering from divided
loyalties. As was only natural, my main sympathies were
with the Jordanians but I had many friends on the other
side. My uneasiness was enhanced because, for the first
time in my long period of public service, in Jordan and
elsewhere, I felt it difficult to defend the policies of my
chiefs in London. In fact, by this time, I was so irritated
by the lunacy which seemed to prevail everywhere that I
sought mental refuge with Lewis Carroll and fitted it all
into *Alice in Wonderland* or *Through the Looking Glass.*
My physical fitness was preserved by the usual week-end
shoots which I kept up regularly, war or no war. It was
not callousness on my part but sheer self defence. I had
lived through two world wars and a great deal of civil

disturbance in the period between them, but conditions were now more trying than they had ever been before.

I was unhappy because after the imposition of the embargoes, I found that I was no longer taken into the complete confidence of the King and the Prime Minister. They appeared to be as friendly as ever but I could no longer depend on being consulted by them before they acted on important issues. It was notable that the King, who had frequently sought consolation from me during the times of the Second World War, did not often discuss developments in Palestine with me of his own volition.

My difficult situation was not eased by the belief, which was commonly held, that, although I was technically nothing more than the head of a foreign diplomatic mission, I somehow still possessed the power as British Resident in the Colonial Service, to compel the Jordanian government to do what I wanted. As a result, I was regarded as being responsible for what the Jordanians did or omitted to do, although, in point of fact, my erstwhile power had slumped to its lowest level ever. Nevertheless, consular officers and officials of the United Nations Organisation continued to call on me to further whatever particular ends they had in view. I could not refuse to receive people of these categories but, for obvious reasons, evaded interviews with representatives of the press as far as was politic.

Although I had a wide acquaintanceship amongst the leaders of the Palestine Arabs, few of them came to see me during the period of the hostilities, and I did not seek them out. During the days of the mandate most of them had expressed confidence in their ability to overcome their opponents if only the interfering British would get out of the ring. One of them had told me that he would dance with joy if we left Palestine. Now that we had gone and left them to face the realities of the situation, they were furious at being left in the lurch. Not only had they decided that the British Government could no longer do them any good, but many of them disapproved of the plans which King Abdullah had for the future of Arab Palestine. In their minds, I was too closely associated with the King to be cultivated separately. I had no contact of any description with Israeli quarters once hostilities commenced. The British connection was so unpopular with the Arabs at that time that the discovery of any such link would have had disastrous results; so disastrous that I did not consider the risk worth taking.

One of my most important diplomatic callers during this period was Count Folke Bernadotte who had been appointed Mediator by the Secretary General of the United Nations Organisation. Unfortunately, my cook was taken ill just before lunch on the day of the first visit to my house and the tête-à-tête meal was not worthy of the occasion. We talked at length but I did not see much more of him afterwards, either because he had remembered the poor food or because he had accepted at their face value my assurances that my influence, which he desired to use, was not all that it had been. However, he got on well with Glubb, which was important.

The first task which Bernadotte set himself was to secure a truce and he succeeded in arranging for one of four weeks duration to commence on June 11th 1948. Apart from the Lebanese and the Jordanians, the Arab governments were not keen on halting the hostilities. They still held the initiative and, on the whole, appeared to be winning the war. The exaggerated reports of the favourable positions of the Arab armies put out by the Arabic press and radio services made the Arab League all the more reluctant to accept the proposed cease-fire. The Lebanese and the Jordanians, on the other hand, had never wanted to start the fight and they were only too ready to stop it: but they could not afford to say so.

The Arab Legion was in great need of a breathing space which would give Glubb and his colleagues an opportunity of bringing forward partly trained men to fill the gaps in the ranks due to the heavy losses sustained by the Legion in the fighting in Jerusalem. The proportion of the casualties had been too high for a force of its size. There was no lack of new recruits for the Legion but the time needed to turn them into soldiers was in a woefully short supply, as was the money needed to meet the cost of the army's increase in manpower.

The Mediator did more than secure a pause in the fighting. He produced the outlines of a settlement of the Palestine problem which was, in essence, a variation of King Abdullah's scheme for a Semitic Kingdom. It seems probable that Bernadotte may have been inspired by what was said during his talks with the King. The basis of the new plan was some form of union or federation between Jordan and Israel. The complete fusion of the two states was not contemplated because each of them would continue to administer its internal affairs independently of the other, subject to co-operation in foreign policy, defence and economics. It was suggested that the Arabs should take the Negev in exchange for western Galilee, that Jerusalem should be Arab and that there should be free zones at Haifa port and Lydda airport. The proposals concerning the city of Jerusalem and the Negev damned the plan in Jewish eyes prior to any discussion. The Jordanian government would have liked to use the ideas as a basis for negotiation but, once again, they were not free to voice their feelings. The other Arab belligerents were unanimous in their opposition to the scheme because they were committed publicly to the destruction of Israel and because they were against any solution which would enhance the position of King Abdullah.

My own opinion was that the idea would not have worked in practice because, like the earlier partition scheme, it called for a degree of co-operation between the Jews and the Arabs which was neither possible at that time or likely to be so within the foreseeable future. All that the proposals did was to lead to the assassination of Bernadotte by Jewish extremists on September 17th and his suggestions died with him.

In the meantime, the next step of the Mediator was

to propose a prolongation of the truce for an indefinite period. It was hardly necessary to use persuasion to induce King Abdullah and the Jordanian Ministers to agree to the extension. Both the King and the Prime Minister were shrewd enough to realise that the Arab armies had just about shot their bolts. Superficially, the Arab positions appeared to be more favourable than they were in reality. It was true that their forces had captured the Jewish quarter in the Old City of Jerusalem and had driven out the inhabitants of the Jewish settlements in the hills of Judea; that their first advance had carried their forward elements to the outskirts of Tel Aviv, but they had now come up against the hard core of Israeli resistance. On the other hand, the Arabs were running short of ammunition and were overstretching their lines of communication. There was also the psychological effect on the rank and file of the Arab armies of the discovery that the campaign was not to be the triumphant walkover which they were led to expect at the outset. Finally, there was the growing realisation that the Israelis were much more successful in evading the international measures which were taken to prevent military supplies reaching the combatants.

It would undoubtedly have been in the best interests of the Arabs had the truce been prolonged and they had then pressed for the implementation of the scheme of partition with amendments in their favour. At the meeting of Arab Prime Ministers convened to consider the matter, Tewfiq abul Huda went to represent Jordan, with every intention of agreeing to the continuation of the ceasefire. He had reason to suppose that Nokrashy Pasha, the Premier of Egypt, would follow the same policy but, in the event, the latter made a strong speech in favour of the resumption of the fighting with the result that the vote in rejecting Bernadotte's proposal was unanimous. Once again, the Jordanians did not feel able to take an independent line. Tewfiq felt that Nokrashy was no fool and was perfectly aware of the facts of the situation; he thought that his Egyptian colleague was probably an unwilling prisoner of the powerful propaganda machinery of his own country which gave the world such glowing accounts of the imaginary glorious victories and prophesied the imminent capture of Tel Aviv. Nokrashy simply could not afford to risk his political future by admitting that he wanted a truce.

Rather to the general surprise, King Abdullah was invited to pay official visits to Egypt and Saudi Arabia during the truce. There must have been some ulterior motive behind the moves but I never discovered what it was. The King was reticent on his return to Amman and would only say that he had had a nice time and that his hosts had not failed in their duties as such. To me this meant that the visit had not been a great success and I suspected that, as was usually the case, the King had voiced too many truths which proved unpalatable to the other leaders.

King Abdullah made no secret of his reluctance to recommence active operations and the other Arab national chiefs decided to offer him an incentive to show more zeal, by appointing him Commander-in-Chief of the Arab armies in the field. He accepted the honour gracefully but he was soon to discover how empty it was. His orders were only executed by his own troops and, when he proposed that he should make a tour of inspection and encouragement of the front line of the Egyptian Army, he was told bluntly that the time was not convenient for him to do so. After that snub, he took typically clever means of demonstrating that he realised his true position by attending a subsequent meeting of Arab heads of states, held at Deraa on the Syrian frontier with Jordan, dressed in the uniform of a private soldier of the Arab Legion. When a much bemedalled Syrian general had the impertinence to remark that he was under the impression that the King was a Field Marshal, the King had said, 'The most honourable rank which I possess is that of an Arab warrior'. The point was taken and the pretence that he was in charge was dropped.

Apart from being exercises in nationalistic oratory, these summit meetings meant so little in practical results that I ceased to take much interest in their proceedings. Their irrelevance made them modern versions of Alice's adventures. Indeed, the general set-up merged more and more into the crazy background of that fantasy. The King was endlessly busy trying to induce other members of the cast to be reasonable; the Prime Minister, like the Black Queen, was running hard to stay where he was and the Minister of Foreign Affairs, like the White Queen, believed a number of impossible things every day before breakfast. There was a large assortment of Knaves and March Hares to choose from, and although we did not yet have a Duchess or a White Rabbit, those missing characters were to appear in due course.

CHAPTER 4

Lydda and Ramleh

The greater part of the actions fought during the years 1948 and 1949 between the Arab Legion and the Israeli Army were bound up, more or less directly, with the possession of Jerusalem or with access to that city. Once the positions of the two forces inside Jerusalem were stabilised before the commencement of the first truce, it was a foregone conclusion that the Israelis' next move would be to endeavour to establish road communications between Jerusalem and Tel Aviv along which they would be able to pass supplies and reinforcements. It was equally predictable that the Arab Legion would have to try and deny that objective to their opponents by establishing themselves in force across the mouth of the defile at Latrun through which the principal road from the coast to the highlands of Judea passed. The situation was a curious reversal of that which existed during the early history of the Israelites when they had been in occupation of the mountain areas and had fought against the Philistines who were established on the maritime plain.

During the first pause in the fighting, Glubb had discussed the situation with me, assuming that the truce would not endure. He had expressed the view that his command would be over-extended if it had to prepare for a major battle in the foot-hills in addition to holding on to its strategic anchor at Ramallah, and, at the same time, preserving the all important political situation in Jerusalem. We were driven to the unavoidable conclusion, however, that the loss of Latrun or failure to defend the place, would probably render the Arab Legion's position in Jerusalem untenable. As he rose to leave my office, Glubb remarked with feeling, 'Well, there will be nothing phoney about the war which will follow the termination of the truce'. Events proved him to be right.

The decision of the Arab leaders to resume active operations had been coupled with the impracticable proviso that they would only fight on the defensive. The effect of their attempts to remain on the defensive resulted in their losing to the other side the precious initiative which they had hitherto held. Given all these circumstances, it was highly probable that the first move of the Israelis in the central front after the end of the truce, would be to attack the two towns of Lydda and Ramleh which sprawled across the road between Tel Aviv and Latrun. The capture of those towns was an essential preliminary to an offensive against the main Arab position at Latrun which barred the way to Jerusalem.

Although the principal airport of the country was situated in Lydda, the Jordanian government had realised from the outset that it was not feasible for them to hold Lydda and Ramleh against a serious attack. The main Israeli base at Tel Aviv was dangerously close and the wide built-up areas of the two towns would need more troops to defend them than the Arab Legion could make available. It was decided, therefore, not to appoint a military governor, as had been done elsewhere, but to allow the two municipalities to exercise the administrative authority which was needed to keep the wheels of government turning. The authorities at Amman felt that the loss of the centres might be less damaging to their prestige if they had never formally established their authority there.

The townsmen raised their own contingents of Fighters who were armed with a curious assortment of more or less serviceable rifles, but the elders did not show much confidence in their guards and they begged the Jordanian command to send them an adequate garrison of regular troops. These pleas for support were met, during the truce, by the arrival of a couple of hundred bedouin volunteers from Jordan and a company of infantry numbering about a hundred men, detached with great reluctance from the force holding the trenches at Latrun. It was not imagined that these reinforcements would secure the safety of the towns, and the reason of their provision was merely to silence the importunities of the inhabitants. The much vaunted ability of the Arabs to drive out the Jews with sticks had been shattered by the loss of the cities· of Jaffa and Haifa almost without resistance by the Arab citizens.

The engagement of volunteers from the nomadic tribes of the east bank was a piece of improvisation inspired by King Abdullah with the idea of using fighting men unsuitable for enlistment in the army, to bolster up the front line strength of the troops. The men in question had no military training and, like all people of that category, however brave they might have been individually, were virtually useless when pitted against proper soldiers. I stood in my garden at Amman and watched one of their first parties passing through in hired civilian lorries on their way to the front. Their ages varied from grey-beards to striplings and they all appeared to be in high spirits. They were singing their war songs and keeping up a *feu-de-joie* from their rifles which must have dissipated the greater part of the precious ammunition with which they had been issued, long before they saw an Israeli. They proved to be unqualified nuisances for whom the townspeople were not a bit grateful, but they had a wonderful time for as long as the truce lasted. They were lodged and fed at the expense of the municipalities and they amused themselves by raiding the Israeli lines for loot; some of them were not above helping themselves to any Arab property which they found unguarded. The instinctive dislike and suspicion which poisons relations between Arab nomads and town dwellers was, I have no doubt, responsible for part of the trouble and friction which occurred at Lydda and Ramleh. In such circumstances, no effective defence was possible and, when the Israeli attack materialised, the tribesmen fired off most of their remaining rounds of ammunition and then faded away into the darkness, after the manner of their kind, carrying their swag on their backs.

The Israeli assault started on July 9th twenty-four hours after the expiration of the truce, and Lydda and Ramleh were in their hands by the 12th of the month. The Arabs put up little resistance; the Fighters fell into confusion and dispersed and the infantry company, whose commander had been ordered to avoid loss of personnel, also withdrew under cover of the night when he judged that his tiny force could do nothing more to save the two towns from capture. The soldiers made their way back on foot to their companions at Latrun. They marched amidst a horde of refugees.

Many of the original wave of refugees from Jaffa who had ended their first flight at Lydda or Ramleh in the hope that they would be able to return to their homes before long, now resumed their wandering in company with most of the population of those towns and that of the surrounding villages. A flood of displaced persons spread across Palestine into Jordan; those with the least means were the first to come to a standstill and only those who were sufficiently well off to possess a motor car, or to hire one, got as far as Amman.

I was standing in the main square of the capital as the tide of miserable humanity reached there. The newcomers drove in, stopped their cars and sat there with blank faces waiting for somebody to do something. One man who had a loudspeaker attached to his car, made a long appeal for aid in a wailing voice and, as he complained about their having been driven from their homes, I wondered how many of them could have stayed where they had been living had they had a little more courage.

Two Armenian friends of ours, who had fled from Jerusalem where they had had a shoemakers business, had told me that they had run away from the Arab quarter in which they had lived when the other inhabitants had panicked. They admitted that they had not even seen an Israeli.

The refugees from Lydda and Ramleh were not the first to arrive in Jordan, but the proportions of the latest influx took the people of the East Bank aback. The authorities at Amman had not made preparations to deal with anything approaching such numbers but the inhabitants, although stunned by the disaster, rallied round in a most commendable fashion and, by nightfall, all the new arrivals had been provided with shelter of some sort, mainly in private dwellings.

Up to that time, the press and radio services of the Arab world had been entirely optimistic about the progress of the war and its probable outcome. Now, the general euphoria generated by the inaccuracies of those media became counter-productive: when a major setback could no longer be concealed, it had to be explained away by accusing somebody of treachery. Therefore, the otherwise inexplicable loss of the two towns was described as a sell-out by the British with Mr Ernest Bevin as the man principally responsible. King Abdullah, the friend and puppet of Great Britain, came next in the order of demerit with Glubb as runner-up. The refugees in Jordan seemed to make the unfortunate Glubb their particular target for abuse, and he and his men, from being popular heroes, turned almost overnight into the villains of the piece. Children spat at Glubb's armed convoy as he drove through the streets and my own car, flying a small union jack, attracted scowls and shaking fists. Thank goodness, nothing more lethal than gestures and grimaces came my way.

There were some ugly mass protest demonstrations in the streets of Amman and Irbid in the days which followed the withdrawal of the Arab Legion to the Latrun lines.

I was paying a call at the palace one morning, when a couple of thousand Palestinian men swept up the hill towards the main entrance of the royal residence, screaming abuse and demanding that the lost towns should be reconquered at once. Men of the royal bodyguard turned out thrusting clips of cartridges into the magazines of their rifles and it seemed to me that a blood-bath was imminent. Then, the King appeared at the top of the main steps of the building; he was a short dignified figure wearing white robes and headdress. He paused for a minute surveying the seething mob before walking down the steps to push his way through the line of guardsmen into the thick of the demonstrators. He went up to a prominent individual, who was shouting at the top of his voice, and dealt him a violent blow to the side of the head with the flat of his hand. The recipient of the blow stopped yelling and, in the relative silence which fell, the King could be heard roaring: 'So, you want to fight the Jews, do you? Very well, there is a recruiting office for the army at the back of my house. Those of you who really want to fight, go there and enlist. The rest of you get the hell down the hillside!' Most of the crowd got to hell down the hillside, amidst cries of 'God give our Lord Victory'. A few of the men actually went and enlisted.

This sort of incident deepened the concern for the King's safety which the Ministers and I felt during this period. There were constant rumours of current plots against his life and, while many of the stories were probably without foundation, there were powerful forces intent on his destruction. There had been one proven attempt on his life which had been nipped in the bud by the vigilance of the guard, and there had been another affair which had misfired through the alertness of an Iraqi officer.

In the first instance, a man was spotted and arrested while he was lying with a loaded rifle in his hand, in some bushes overlooking the road running down from Amman to the Jordan Valley where the King had his winter quarters. Under suitable pressure, the suspect had admitted to having been bribed by a Syrian officer to shoot the King as he drove past.

The second attempt had been more complicated and might easily have been fatal. Whilst driving down the same road, an Iraqi staff officer had noticed a pair of wires running from the edge of the road up the hillside, where there had been no reason for the wires to be. He had stopped his car and closer investigation had revealed a charge of explosive matter buried in the berm of the road with the wires already connected to a detonator and leading up to a hidden place behind some boulders, where they were ready to be attached to an electric exploder. The mine had been situated at a point where the road ran round a sharp curve with a sheer drop of several hundred feet on the other side of the track. It had evidently been the intention to blast the royal car over the side of the precipice.

The police investigators had never succeeded in establishing the identities of those responsible for organising these two attempts but the most popular belief was that they had been carried out by disgruntled refugees in the pay of the Syrian or Egyptian governments.

Efforts to safeguard the sovereign were intensified but they were made more difficult by his insistence on being accessible to all his subjects and to his disregard for danger which stemmed from his fatalism. He believed unquestioningly in the predestination of men and no amount of persuasion would induce him to bother much about our precautionary measures. To illustrate his way of thinking, he liked to tell of a story about a man named Abdul Aziz who lived in Basrah when there was an outbreak of plague in Iraq. For a while, the man watched his neighbours sicken and die, then he decided to try and escape infection by going to the country-side. He and his wife loaded their most precious possessions on a donkey and slipped out of the city gate one day at dawn. After walking for a few hours, they stopped to rest and the woman fell asleep; as they sat, the man heard a voice say in his ear, 'Oh Abdul Aziz, you cannot outstrip death on a donkey'. He hesitated for time, then he awakened his wife and started to walk back to their home city.

The Israeli advance which overran the towns of Lydda and Ramleh was the first phase of a drive to eject the Arab Legion from their hold at Latrun on the key road to Jerusalem. The effort was continued with undiminished determination until the very eve of the second truce but the Arab position held and the offensive was thrown back. The men on both sides fought with equal gallantry and suffered substantial losses in casualties. Even the bedouin volunteers, who had done so poorly at Ramleh, redeemed their reputation fighting beside their kinsmen in one of the bedouin regiments. The successful stand at Latrun was the last major Arab gain and looking back, it is evident that the tide turned against them after the end of the first truce.

I felt a special sympathy during the fighting around Latrun for the community of Trappist monks whose monastery and beautiful orchards stood only a few yards behind the police post which was the focal point of the Israeli onslaught. I had spent a happy week with the fathers in the summer of 1943, when the war weariness had made it imperative for me to go into retreat for a spell. It seemed hard that those admirable men, who had turned their backs on the world, in search of peace, should find themselves in the midst of a battle.

While there had been a certain amount of unison on broad lines amongst the Arabs during the opening moves of the campaign, true co-operation had been lacking at all levels. Instead of improving as the situation developed, the co-operation decreased until there was not even an exchange of military intelligence, let alone co-ordination of military operations. When the Israeli pressure on the Arab garrison in Jerusalem increased, or rather, was renewed, and the Israeli offensive in the foothills had pinned down the main force of the Arab Legion, a request was addressed to the Egyptian commander for his troops to be more active in the vicinity of Bethlehem in order to take the weight off the rest of the front. He declined to comply on the grounds that it might be dangerous for his men to do so. He said to Glubb: 'We might even be attacked, my dear'.

The political rivalry between the various groups of the Fighters in Jerusalem was accentuated by the revival of the fighting there and news of the trouble reached me at Amman. Musa al-Alami, one of the leaders of the party opposed to Haj Amin el-Husseini, called at my house to ask me to arrange for his section of the Fighters to be given supplies of ammunition. By this time, the Arab Legion was the only source of such stores available to the irregular formations. Mr Alami complained that his party had been compelled to purchase cartridges in the bazaar which had actually been issued by the Trans-jordanian authorities to the other section for use in the defence of Jerusalem.

To crown all the other difficulties, it was about this time that Abder Rahman Azzam refused to pay to the Jordanian government, additional funds from the Arab League war chest in spite of his earlier promise to finance the additional cost to Jordan of participation in the war.

The second truce negotiated by Count Bernadotte took effect from July 18th. This time, the stoppage was to be of indefinite duration and the principle upon which its terms were based was that the combatants were permitted to maintain their arms and supplies at their pre-truce level. The difficulty of enforcing a provision of this type was obvious to all concerned.

The Arab leaders needed no prodding to induce them to accept the second ceasefire, but the Israelis were not so sure that they wanted to stop fighting. The latter had kept up the attacks on Latrun until the very last moment and, having failed to gain possession of the existing road to Jerusalem, they quite legitimately used the respite of the second truce to construct an alternate track from the plain which by-passed the Arab defences at Latrun. There was a suitable alignment along a valley to the south of Latrun running through country over which the Arab Legion was unable to extend its control. The completion of the new track enabled the Isarelis to relieve the beleaguered population in Jewish Jerusalem and the Arabs were left in the undisturbed occupation of Latrun which ceased to have any particular strategic significance.

The enforcement of the complicated conditions of the new agreement was a difficult task for the Truce Observation Commission, especially as both sides did their utmost to evade its application. The Israelis proved to be much more efficient in their evasion of the controls, and, amongst other things, they managed to launch an effective little air force during the following few weeks. The breaches of the ceasefire were so frequent that in his book 'A Soldier with the Arabs', Glubb dubbed it the 'Shooting truce'.

The strain of carrying on the war with inadequate resources and unreliable allies was very great on those in authority at Amman. I was acutely unhappy, but my own special worry was that of not being able to do much to help my friends in their hour of need. Sympathy and moral support were not much use to them but they were all that I had to offer. Tempers became frayed and a series of rows between Glubb and the King and the Prime Minister, which were out of character on both sides, indicated the importance for Glubb, who bore the heaviest burden, to get away from Jordan for a while. Advantage was taken of the second pause in the operations to let him take a few weeks' leave with his family in the United Kingdom. Whilst he was in England, Glubb was under constant guard by armed detectives because it was believed that there were both Arab and Jewish organisations planning his assassination. As he remarked, it was a rare distinction to be threatened with death by both sides simultaneously.

King Abdullah gave Glubb a personal letter addressed to Mr Bevin for delivery by hand in London. The message described the plight of Jordan in detail and asked for a mitigation of the order with-holding supplies of money and ammunition. Glubb was given a personal interview by the Foreign Secretary but got no satisfaction from the occasion. Mr Bevin indulged in a long tirade on the subject of the behaviour of the Arabs who had, he said, rewarded his many attempts to assist them with abuse and ingratitude; he admitted that the Jordanians were not as bad as some of the others but could not give them preferential treatment. He did not send a written reply to the King's letter.

My staff and I worked hard during this time but those of us who were most affected by the additional work were the cypher officers and the operators who manned the mobile wireless station which linked me directly with the Foreign Office and most of the other diplomatic posts in the Middle East. This station was a curse and a blessing at one and the same time. On occasion, it was useful to be able to get information through to London in the space of a few minutes but it was not so pleasant when other posts deluged us with top secret and urgent cypher messages at all hours of the day and night. So many of these telegrams urged some action or other on my part or by the Jordanian government, that one doubted whether the independence of the Hashemite Kingdom of Jordan was always taken at its face value.

This telegraphic advice rarely caught up with events and, in the end, it was arranged that repetitions of such signals to and from London should be circulated to other posts by means of the diplomatic bags.

There seemed to be no end to the oddity of the things which I and my staff were obliged to deal with. It was evident that any one who was at a loss as to what to do, turned automatically to the British Legation. On two separate occasions taxis from Jerusalem had driven up to the door unheralded and had presented us with a corpse to be disposed of. Both the dead men had been soldiers who were serving with the corps of United Nations

Observers stationed in Palestine. The first of them, a Swede, presented no problem and was buried in the Protestant cemetery but the other, who was a Hindu sepoy, was more difficult to dispose of. No letters arrived with the corpses but the taxi drivers, who were instructed simply to deliver their cargoes to the British Legation, explained that there was no cemetery available in Jerusalem in which members of their sects could be buried. Experts told us that the Indian should be cremated so we rose to the occasion and borrowed the use of the municipal incinerator for an afternoon.

During the summer of 1948, there was no material change in the front line positions held by the various Arab armies, save that the Army of Deliverance handed over their positions in the Samaritan hills partly to the Iraqi army and partly to the Arab Legion and moved to the areas of Galilee which were without garrison. The line of the Army of Deliverance had been a series of outposts manned by men armed with small arms and it had been clear that they would have been incapable of repelling a serious attack. The order for a changeover came from the Arab League where it was probably felt that Providence could be tempted no longer. Fawzi el-Kaowkji was unabashed, however, and when he had handed over to officers of the Arab Legion, he had the impertinence to express to Lash the hope that he would guard the sacred homeland as effectively as he had done.

While the Lebanese and Syrian contingents had hardly proceeded beyond their own frontiers in the original advance and had failed to improve their positions since then, they had contributed their quota to the innumerable breaches to the ceasefire orders. According to the United Nations Observers, who should have known, the Israeli complaints of alleged breaches outnumbered those made by the Arabs by the ratio of five to one. As someone remarked at the time, this fact proved nothing except that the Israelis were more vocal than the Arabs.

On September 17th, Count Bernadotte and Colonel
Serot, his French Chief of Staff, were shot and killed
in Jerusalem by Jewish terrorists. Those responsible did
not conceal their identities and took the trouble to
announce that the shooting of the French officer had been
a tragic mistake due to his being mistaken for someone
else. Glubb learned about the murders in Paris while on
his way back to Amman.

The failure of the United Nations Organisation, or anybody else, to take any effective action against the killers,
seemed to result in a marked reluctance on the part of
the members of the corps of observers to take a strong
line on anything connected with their duties and both
the Israelis and the Arabs soon came to realise that nothing drastic would be done by that organisation whatever
infringement of the rules occurred.

The choice of personalities for appointment as the new
Mediator was interesting. Bernadotte, the European
aristocrat, was replaced by Dr Ralph Bunche, an American negro whose grandfather had been a slave. Although
the assassination had weakened the authority of the international organisation, the newcomer had acquired, in a
short period of time, more personal influence in Arab
circles than had been enjoyed by his predecessor. This
was a paradoxical state of affairs, considering that Bernadotte had been killed because of his bias in the favour
of the Arabs, while Bunche avoided showing any favour
to either side. The explanation probably lay in the innate
distrust of most Arabs for any European which predis-
poses the former to be less suspicious when they are dealing with a member of another branch of the human race.

CHAPTER 5

The Government of All-Palestine

King Abdullah had moved into Jordan for the first time in 1921 with the avowed intention of reconquering from the French the Syrian kingdom which had been lost by his brother Faisal. Circumstances had prevented his making any such attempt and had compelled him to accept the lesser prize of the principality of Transjordan. He had always felt that his state was too small to afford him the international scope which he deserved and, from the first day, he had cherished ambitions to widen his domain. His endeavours persisted until the day of his death.

His first priority had been to create a Greater Syria which included both Syria and Jordan but he had been quite prepared to annex Palestine or as much of that country as he could get, in part satisfaction. The Greater Syria project had never been within the realm of practical politics not only because of the opposition of the French Government but also because of the objection of most of the Syrians to having their country taken over by a lesser state inhabited by nomads whom they considered to be a backward people. The King had made a special effort about Syria when the French mandate had been terminated at the end of the Second World War, but without success. The younger generations of Syrians had shown themselves for the most part to be republicans.

The end of the British mandate had been seen by the King as a golden opportunity for acquiring part of Palestine and, as I have already said, he had never concealed his intention of taking over that part of the country which had been allotted to the Arabs in the partition scheme. His Majesty's Government had never liked the Syrian project but they had not discouraged his aims in Palestine.

The other Arab national leaders were practically unanimous in their opposition to King Abdullah's aspirations and the principal reason for their hostility was his notorious friendship for Great Britain. At the time, most Arab statesmen were engaged in the process of undermining British influence in the Middle East and they could hardly be expected, in the circumstances, to look with favour on an Arab King who was doing his best to bolster a dying foreign imperialism. It was also known that he had been in touch with the Jewish leaders and that they were not opposed to his taking over control of Arab Palestine. The apparent preference of the Israelis for Jordan as a neighbour was particularly damning.

Two other factors worked against the King. The first, was that his family provided a dynasty for Iraq, a state which was then Egypt's main competitor for the leadership of the Arab world. The second factor was the rising flood of republicans amongst the younger generation of the Arabs which was shortly to topple King Faruq and some other Arab monarchs from their thrones.

Finally, considerable jealousy surrounded the exploits of the Arab Legion. In spite of the hullabaloo which was raised over the loss of Lydda and Ramleh, most responsible Arabs knew in their hearts that the soldiers of the Legion had done better than the other Arab armies, and had been, in fact, the only ones to score real success in battle over the Israeli forces. What made the realisation hard to swallow was the answer to the question as to what the Legion had which the other Arab armies did not have, which was of course 'British officers'.

The Egyptian and Syrian statesmen were particularly determined that, as far as they were concerned, no benefit should accrue to King Abdullah, whatever the outcome of the conflict in Palestine, and they concocted a plot to that end which was sprung by the Arab League on September 22nd 1948, without the prior knowledge of the Jordanians. The creation was announced of a Government, with its seat at Gaza, exercising jurisdiction over the whole of Palestine. The new administration was to be called the Government of All-Palestine. The Arab League invited the formal recognition of the new state by all other countries and called upon all Palestinians to give it their allegiance.

It was noticeable that the members of the Gaza Government were mostly supporters of the Mufti of Jerusalem, certainly none of whom were friends of the Hashemites. I knew two of the Ministers, the Chairman, Ahmed Hilmi, and the Director of Public Security, Faiz al Idrisi. The former was a banker by profession, without prior administrative experience, who was born in Palestine but came of Bosnian stock who had migrated from Macedonia after the Balkan wars. The latter had been a deputy district superintendent of the Palestine Police. He blossomed into a Major General as soon as he took up the Gaza post and, on the strength of having achieved that exalted rank, was appointed head of the Federal Police of Libya for a brief period.

The newcomers had no funds, no armed forces and no civil services; they only administered the tiny enclave round the town of Gaza by permission of the Egyptian Government. They were entirely dependent on the Egyptians for funds, supplies and protection. In spite of the efforts of their sponsors, there was little popular enthusiasm for the new Government. It was not that the Palestinians did not want to have a government of their own but the Gaza version was too obviously a collection of stooges. King Abdullah and his Ministers treated the move as a joke. Some of the Arab states went through the motion of formal recognition, but His Majesty's Government and other powers followed the lead set by the United Nations Organisation and ignored the so-called Government of All-Palestine.

At this time, doubtless on instructions from Cairo, the Mufti's supporters in Palestine adopted an attitude openly hostile to Jordan and commenced organising another armed force which they called the Holy War Army. One would have thought that there was already a sufficient variety of armies in the field but, when the new formation declined to play any part in the defence of Jerusalem, it became evident that it was going to be used for subversive purposes. Its growth was then nipped in the bud when orders were given by the Jordanian Government that armed bodies operating in the areas controlled by the Arab Legion were either to be under their orders or be disbanded. The Holy War Army refused to submit to this direction and it was forcibly disbanded and dispersed on October 3rd. The plot had failed to achieve its objective but its authors, the Egyptians, had, typically enough, brought the Arabs within measurable distance of fighting amongst themselves whilst still facing an enemy who was growing in strength. A renewed Israeli offensive at that moment might have left the Arab Legion engaging them in the front and being attacked from behind by the Mufti's men.

The appearance of Ahmed Hilmi's cabinet led to some difficulty arising between myself and my Turkish colleague at Amman, a certain Monsieur Shaman. When the latter took up his post, he told me that his chiefs in Ankara had assured him that the British at Amman and I myself, were fully aware of what was going on and would keep him fully posted. I did not tell him everything that I knew, but I did give him preferential treatment in view of Turkey's membership of the North Atlantic Treaty Organisation. His demands for news became so insatiable

that they made me suspect that he was passing on intelligence which I gave him, to the King and was probably
getting paid for his trouble. My suspicions were confirmed
when some particular remark which I had made to him
about the Government of All-Palestine was repeated to
me, word for word, as something which had been said
by the King to the Prime Minister. The discovery of this
duplicity irked me so much that I started feeding false
information to Shaman and, sure enough, some of its
echoes came back to me from the palace. The King was
too shrewd and well informed to fail to realise what was
happening. He reacted, ungratefully, by getting the Prime
Minister to suggest through the Jordanian representative
in Ankara that Shaman's tour of office at Amman might
be terminated with advantage. Before very long notice of
the transfer of my colleague to Madrid came through
from Turkey.

By the middle of October, the Egyptians had more
urgent matters than the thwarting of King Abdullah's
ambitions to occupy their minds. The first advance of
the Arab forces had brought the Egyptian contingent to
a line running across the maritime plain from Isdud, on
the coast, through Falluja to Beit Jibreen in the foothills
and thence up to Bethlehem. Behind this lay a number
of Jewish settlements which had been by-passed and which
had successfully resisted subsequent attempts by the Egyptian troops to carry them by storm. The fact that the
second truce was based on the rule that the supply position
everywhere should be maintained at its previous level,
entitled the Israelis to send periodical convoys of supplies
to the beleaguered garrisons in southern Palestine under
the supervision of the United Nations Observers. On
October 15th one of these convoys was sent forward to
the Egyptian lines without the prescribed United Nations
escort and, when it was fired upon, the Israelis
launched a major attack on the Egyptian troops for which
their forces had been assembled secretly in advance. The
newly fledged Israeli air force participated in this operation

and attacked the Egyptian air fields at Mejdel, Gaza and El Arish.

The Egyptian formations were taken by surprise and they suffered also from the faulty disposition of their commander who showed signs of what might be called a Maginot mentality. The troops were posted in a long line of static defences which consisted mainly of trenches; none of the units were mobile and there did not appear to be any reserve near enough at hand to take part in the battle. Numerically, the two armies were about the same strength but the Egyptians were dispersed at length while the Israelis were concentrated on one point of attack and could burst through the defence without difficulty. As the frontal attack developed, the Israeli garrisons placed to the rear of the Egyptians emerged from their lines and disrupted the enemy lines of communications starting with the railway which was blown up. The whole of the Egyptian front collapsed and, as it was put in a contemporary report, the Egyptian commander simultaneously lost control of himself and the situation.

The Security Council issued its usual call for another ceasefire and secured one which became effective at three o'clock in the afternoon of October 22nd. By the time the fighting came to a halt, the Egyptian forces had been split into two halves. On the plain, all the territory in Palestine was lost except a small enclave round the township of Gaza and an isolated bastion at Falluja where a number of survivors, most of them Sudanese and amounting to about two thousand five hundred men, held out. Falluja was an undistinguished village but its name will go down in history as the place where a young Egyptian officer of field rank, named Jamal Abdel Nasser, gained a well deserved reputation for bravery. The Egyptian garrisons at Hebron and Bethlehem were cut off from their base and the main body of their army which had retreated south into Sinai. They could, to the advantage of their cause, have continued the fight in conjunction with the Arab Legion, but their commanders refused to consider that possibility and they all made their way home to Egypt via Amman and Aqaba.

This débacle left the southern wing of the Jordanian forces in mid air and there was an imminent danger of an Israeli advance on Hebron which, if successful, could have turned the flank of the whole position of the Arab Legion in the Judean mountains.

The Government of All-Palestine dealt with the crisis by taking flight to Cairo and leaving their temporary capital at Gaza packed tight with refugees from the outlying villages in addition to the original population.

Having failed to assist others when Jerusalem was in danger, the Egyptians now clamoured for help. Representatives of the belligerent Arab states who did not include any representation from Gaza met at Amman to consider how best to rescue the Egyptians from their plight. The first speaker was the Prime Minister of Egypt, Nokrashy Pasha, who complained bitterly that no one had raised a finger to help his troops. The next was Jamil Mardam, the Premier of Syria, who, like Alice's white knight, always had a lot to say which sounded impressive, but somehow failed to make sense.

Although the Syrian Army had made no contribution of value to the campaign so far, Jamil Mardam was critical of the other countries for their lack of activity and he promised that, if fighting broke out again, an infantry division of the Syrian Army would gallantly burst into Palestine between the lakes of Huleh and Tiberias and occupy the centre of Galilee. His listeners were not impressed and the Iraqi chief of staff felt able to remark that, if the Syrians really did what they promised, his troops would also march forward and would link with the Syrians by stretching across the plain of Esdraelon. The general themes of the meeting were regret that no one had helped the Egyptians more in the past, determination that they would all do so in the future and relief that it was unnecessary to do so immediately because there was a cease-fire in force. They were all back in

Wonderland again and their resolutions had no practical outcome.

The fact that they had agreed to a ceasefire of the Egyptian front did not inhibit the Israelis from continuing to fire elsewhere and October 28th they turned on the positions of the Army of Deliverance in Galilee. The irregulars won the ensuing race for the frontier of the Lebanon by a few lengths and that was the last that was heard of them and their commander. The pursuers remained in occupation of a strip of Lebanese territory and the fighting on that part of the front line was over for the duration of that particular war.

On the same date, the anticipated move by the Israelis against Hebron materialised and a spirited action was fought between that town and Beit Jibrin in which the Arab Legion prevailed and the Israelis fell back to the plain.

At the end of the month, the situation had changed disastrously for the Arabs in general and the Jordanians in particular. The Egyptians had been knocked out of the fight, the Army of Deliverance had disappeared, the Lebanese and the Syrians had been reduced to impotence and the Iraqis had developed a marked reluctance to becoming involved in active operations. The Arab Legion had been left holding far more land than was safe for a force of its numbers. It was desperately short of artillery ammunition, so much so, that when another appeal for help was made to His Majesty's Government, the latter relented to the extent of authorising the issue of a quantity of barbed wire with which to meet the Israeli offensive. It was carefully explained that wire was a purely defensive article.

The Security Council made a half-hearted attempt to get all the armies back into the positions which they held prior to the breach of the ceasefire but the Israelis refused to comply and nothing more was done in New York. We never knew whether Mr Bevin was trying to help Jordan or whether it was just a question of his taking a long time to reach a decision, but he suddenly announced in the House of Commons that General Glubb was not, after all, liable under the terms of the Foreign Enlistment Act to imprisonment for serving in a foreign army, which was at war, without the cognizance of His Majesty's Government.

In spite of vast reverses, the confidence of the Arab League in victory purported to remain unshaken but a sign of tottering faith came when the Egyptian Minister for Defence sent a personal message to King Abdullah suggesting that the time had come for the king to advise King Faruq that the Arabs should make peace on the best terms obtainable. Taking into account the persistent attacks which had been made from Egyptian sources impugning the King's readiness to prosecute the war as actively as he should, this blatant attempt to trick him into taking a step which no Arab politician could do with impunity, was a colossal piece of impudence and it was treated as such.

In the meanwhile, the problem of the refugees in Jordan was getting out of hand. The loss of so much land to the Israelis during the autumn brought a fresh wave of homeless and destitute folk into a country, which was already overcrowded with the earlier arrivals. Of the half million Palestinians who had already left their homes, most had come to Jordan or the west bank which was held by the Arab Legion. Jordan had always been a poor country, dependent for its solvency on financial aid from Great Britain, and the crushing burden of the refugees was now to be carried in the midst of a war and at a time when help from abroad was withheld.

Lesser numbers of refugees had been accepted by Egypt, Syria and the Lebanon, but it was only in Jordan that the Palestinian Arabs were automatically accorded local nationality, with all the rights that its possession implied. In the other countries, the refugees were confined to camps, treated as stateless persons and denied the right to compete for employment in the local labour market.

Those welcomed to Jordanian territory showed little gratitude for the hospitality extended to them and they frequently staged demonstrations in the streets of Amman protesting against failure to reconquer their homeland. Glubb became a particular target for their hatred and his headquarters in Amman were, on more than one occasion, beset by Palestinian children screaming insults at his name.

One of the few consolations during this trying period was the fact that the anticipated Israeli general offensive against the Arab Legion did not materialise. Instead, there was a meeting at Jerusalem, under United Nations auspices, between an Israeli officer called Moshe Dayan, and an Arab Legion delegate by the name of Abdullah el Tel. They were not famous men at the time but the former was to become a Minister in the Israeli Government and the latter was to be implicated three years later, in the murder of his benefactor, King Abdullah. Their meeting was convened to produce what was called a 'real' truce covering Jerusalem. Surprisingly enough, the agreement which emerged was observed to a degree which was not achieved by the earlier ceasefire.

With Jerusalem quiet, Israeli interest switched to the Negev in an ominous manner. The Israelis explained away any troop movements south of the Dead Sea as being purely defensive to meet possible Arab aggression. There were, in fact, no Arab troops in that locality and the general assumption was that the moves were preliminaries to mounting an operation, with the Gulf of Aqaba as the objective.

During this lull in the fighting, the garrison at Falluja declined to take advantage of an opportunity to break through to freedom. A British officer of the Arab Legion, Major Geoffrey Lockett, with a local guide had twice slipped through the Israeli lines near to the Hebron foothills and had made his way on foot to the perimeter at Falluja, a dozen miles away. He had not been cordially received and his offer to guide the garrison to safety under the cover of darkness had been declined. He had received the impression that the beseiged commander had been unable to stomach the disgrace of being indebted to the British and the Jordanians.

If the Egyptians had taken advantage of the opportunity and had broken through, they would have suffered some loss but Glubb had estimated that about eighty percent of the garrison could have escaped. As it was, they continued to hold out until the Egyptian armistice agreement was signed in February of 1949, and they were then able to march out honourably. Perhaps they had been right to refuse to move before.

Given this respite, King Abdullah decided that it was safe for him to proceed with his plan to annex what was left of Arab Palestine. The same objection to being taken over by a lesser country of nomads, which had been responsible for the opposition of the Syrians to union with Jordan, had been felt by many people of Palestine whose national aim was to achieve the status of an independent state. So long, therefore, as there was any hope of an Arab victory, the atmosphere was not favourable to the fulfillment of an act of union. After the Egyptian rout during the month of October, however, no amount of misleading propaganda could conceal the fact that the Arab success which had been promised was an illusion and that, at least for the time being, the creation of an independent Arab state of Palestine was not practical. The Government of All-Palestine was a farce and the land under their jurisdiction was reduced to the Gaza Strip, that is to say, it encompassed little more than a refugee camp.

An inkling of the King's intention to move towards annexation must have reached the authorities in Cairo because Prince Mohammed Ali, who was an old friend of the King, unexpectedly invited himself to lunch at Amman and, when he arrived, made it clear that he intended to talk about Palestine. His coming was an extraordinary démarche; after all, the visitor was still the heir-apparent to the throne of Egypt. I was the only foreign diplomat invited to attend the meal and I was embarrassed by the blatant attempts which were made by both sides to get me to commit myself for or against the union, and presumably the British Government as well. Mohammed Ali had been briefed with a dozen reasons why Jordan should not take over the remnant of Arab Palestine and King Abdullah, on the other hand, was determined not to miss the occasion to widen his domain. Both of them became restive at my elusive replies and the party was not a success. The brotherly embrace given to the guest as he departed was not as cordial as that with which he had been received. The visit and its homilies had no deterrent effect on the King.

The future of the west bank of Jordan was not decided by the whim of the King alone. Many of his most influential supporters, including Tewfiq abùl Huda, were themselves of Palestinian origin and had strong feelings about the fate of their native land. The problem was discussed interminably but one could not get away from the conclusion that what was left of Palestine to the Arabs, was too small and impoverished an area to constitute a viable state, even had there been no refugees there. The west bank held by the Jordanians consisted of the Old City in Jerusalem, the highlands of Samaria and the Judean mountains excluding the salient in Israeli hands which connected Jewish Jerusalem with the maritime plain. In that space, the number of destitute refugees equalled that of the original inhabitants. Moreover, the west bank was landlocked by Israel on one side and Transjordan on the other.

The majority of the Palestinians, including many who had no love for the King, came to the same conclusion as that voiced by the Prime Minister in the course of one of our discussions, namely that, 'Union with Jordan is the only solution at the present time'. After that, the rest of the actions were little more than formalities. On December 1st, the Jordanian government convened a con-

gress of Palestinian leaders at Jericho where a resolution
was passed, almost unanimously, in favour of the union
of Palestine with the Hashemite Kingdom of Jordan. This
decision was accepted by the Transjordanian Parliament
which, in turn, enacted the amendment to the Organic
Law which was required to put the change into effect
immediately. Although the act of union referred to the
whole of Palestine, in practice the Gaza Strip was never
administered by Jordan.

Not only did the inhabitants of the west bank have
their doubts about the proposed settlement; many of the
inhabitants of the east bank viewed the incorporation of
Palestine with misgiving because it turned the old Jordanians into a permanent minority in the new state. After
the union, the proportions of the two sections of the
population was about nine hundred thousand west
bankers to about four hundred and fifty thousand east
bankers.

I do not think that any of us concerned realised at
the time how much the east bank, which had given birth
to the kingdom, was changing as a result of the massive
influx of Palestinians. They came as poor additions to
a poor country, they consumed much of the hitherto
exportable surplus of agricultural produce, they created
a housing shortage and competed with the indigenous
population for the little industrial employment which was
to be found in the urban centres. The effects of the mig-
ration were, however, greatest in the political and social
fields. They had no particular reasons to be loyal to the
ruling dynasty and many of them were republicans
by conviction. They had been affected by the long years
of political frustration into which they had been led by
their chiefs and they were unforgivingly bitter against the
British and the Americans for the ruin which had overtaken all their hopes. For them, their homeland was *terra
irridenta*, a natural fact which made a peace settlement
between Jordan and Israel that much more difficult. On
the social side, after nearly thirty years of subjection to

various European influences in their education, they had lost many of the better traditions and customs of their forefathers and had acquired in exchange a lot of theories which they did not really understand.

Personally, I had been convinced that union was the best solution in the circumstances. The only alternative seemed to be to try and set up a separate state but no one thought that such an idea was practical. I came to wonder whether I had not been mistaken, when I saw the behaviour of the Palestine guerrillas in 1970–71.

The union drove the Egyptian and Syrian politicians into a frenzy of resentment and the Arab League, under their influence passed a decision refusing to recognise the validity of the act. This policy of non-recognition was, of course, followed by the Government of All-Palestine, but with no practical effect whatsoever on the situation in Jordan. His Majesty's Government raised an objection to the step being taken but their formal recognition was withheld until after the conclusion of the armistice.

CHAPTER 6

A Side Show

In the early days of the mandatory regime, when economic co-operation between all sections of the population of Palestine was still a thing to be hoped for, a concession was granted by the Palestinian and Jordanian governments for the extraction of the minerals which were held in suspension in the waters of the Dead Sea. The concessionaires were a firm registered in Great Britain and financed by Jewish owned capital; apart from a few unskilled Arab labourers, the personnel employed on the undertaking were Jewish. The company built evaporation pans at the south end of the Dead Sea, with other pans, a processing plant and a workers' settlement at the northern end of the lake. All the installations were situated in the part of Palestine which was to be allotted to the Arabs in the partition scheme. In the circumstances, although it was technically a British concern, the Palestine Potash Corporation was regarded by the local authorities and the Arabs as being an exclusively Jewish business.

Having regard to the location of its works, it was evident that the corporation would be in difficulties when the end of the mandate came and, as a result of some wire pulling in London, I was instructed in April of 1948, to do what I could to safeguard an asset which was of such potential value to both sides of the Jordan. The

Jordanian Ministers were quite amenable to my representations, notwithstanding the Jewish character of the firm,
and they asked Glubb to inspect the northern works
personally with a view to placing them under Arab
Legion guard. Glubb described his visit as having been
discouraging because he was taken round by the managing
director, Mr M. Novomeisky, followed by an armoured
car manned by men who purported to be auxilliary
members of the Palestine police force but were, more probably, men of the Hagana. The crew of the armoured car
kept a sub-machine gun pointing at Glubb throughout
the whole of the tour. I would not have been as patient
as Glubb, had I been in his place.

The Jordanian government offered to put a police
guard on the installations on condition that all armed
Jewish personnel were first withdrawn. This not unreason-
able proviso was rejected by the corporation and nothing
further happened until the day before the end of the mandate, when all the occupants of the factory and the workers'
settlement were evacuated by boat to the south end of
the sea. The decision to leave must have been unexpected
because when the Jordanian police moved in to take over,
they found meals left standing in the dining halls.

The empty factory and kibbutz were left without a
proper Jordanian guard and looted by the local inhabitants. In a matter of weeks, the valuable machinery was
wrecked irreparably by being used as a mine for scrap-
metal. However, the installations at the south end of the
sea remained in Jewish hands for the duration of the
war; hence this story.

The land round the south end of the Dead Sea, has
very old historical associations. The frontier between
Jordan and Israeli passes through a shallow bay of land
which is probably the Vale of Siddim, referred to in the
book of Genesis, chapter 14, verse 3, of the Old Testament.
The valley is a torrid hole nearly thirteen hundred feet
below the level of the Mediterranean sea; part of it consists
of stretches of swamp and slime, while the rest is covered

with thickets, bushes, tamarisks, thorny acacias and other types of sub-tropical vegetation; its southern lands are watered by perennial streams of fresh water which flow down from the mountains of Moab. At a point known as Es Safi, where one of the largest of the streams debouches from the hills, a police post stands on the summit of an isolated hill on which are situated the ruins of a more ancient settlement. A little further to the west, there is a small modern hamlet inhabited by negroid peasants who farm the fields. The place is, apparently, Zoar of the Bible. I spent some uncomfortable weeks there as a soldier attached to the Arab Army in 1918.

At the western end of the Vale, the works of the corporation stand at the base of Jebel Usdum (Mount Sodom). Adjacent swamps have been adapted to serve as evaporating pans for the extraction of the valuable salts which impregnate the water of the sea. No part of this section of the valley is cultivated and it does not produce any really sweet water.

The Arab armies were too preoccupied elsewhere trying to hold on to more valuable parts of Palestine, to trouble about so remote a spot. Consequently the Jewish garrison of armed workers at the southern works remained undisturbed but short of supplies of fresh meat and vegetables. The only representatives of the Jordanian government in the vicinity were ten men of the urban police section of the Arab Legion who occupied the police post. The peasants were timid unwarlike folk but the Kerak tribesmen, who lived in the hills to the east, were a different proposition and most of the men were armed with rifles of first world war vintage. The tribes, however, had not attempted to interfere with the people in the works at Jebel Usdum.

This calm was shattered one morning, just after dawn in the autumn of 1948, when the occupants of the police post heard a commotion break out in the village and then saw men, women and children running towards them in a panic and screaming, 'The Jews are here. The Jews

are here'. Two constables who were detailed to go out
on foot and investigate the noise, were greeted by a volley
of rifle fire from the intruders in the village and they
returned to their comrades in considerable haste. The Arab
Legion had built a series of posts in a fortress-like pattern
at places likely to be the focus of trouble, but Es Safi
had always been assumed to be a safe place. The post
there was a single storeyed building of mud brick designed
to serve as an office and a barracks but not to resist
an attack by armed men.

The local district administrative headquarters were at
Kerak where I had been President of the National Government of Moab from 1920–21, before the arrival of the
King Abdullah. The distance from Kerak to the post in
danger was only about twenty miles in a straight line
but there was a difference of nearly five thousand feet
in altitude over the precipitous mountains which lay
between the two places. There was a rough track passable
for motor transport which ran northwards from Es Safi
along the eastern shore of the sea to Mezraa before turning
eastwards to climb up to Kerak. The direct route from
the town to the post, could only be used by cars for
a third of its distance, before it plunged down to so steep
and difficult a descent that even the local inhabitants
usually dismounted from pack animals and scrambled
down on their feet.

While the policemen at Es Safi were hurriedly doing
what they could with a few sandbags to improvise
defences, their wireless operator sent off a message to
Kerak giving the alarm and calling urgently for assistance.
Some minutes after despatching the message, the first bullets whistled overhead or smacked into the mud walls
of the post coming from the hedges and bushes which
surrounded the village. The rattle of automatic weapons
could also be distinguished. At first, the garrison who
manned the windows, had two of their number lying on
the flat roof of the building, but the defenders could not
make out the attackers clearly until the latter pushed for-

ward making as though to outflank the post from the rear. The peasants and their families vanished into the bush and were seen no more until the affair was over, but the police were joined by half a dozen Kerak tribesmen. One of the latter was in a very bad temper and was calling for vengeance against the Jews who had captured him in the village and had subjected him to some rough treatment in order to induce him to give information about the number of police who held the post. He had made a successful dash for liberty once action had become general and his guards had become preoccupied with other matters.

No military units of the Arab Legion were available nearer than Amman, a hundred miles away, but on receiving the calls for help, the commandant of the police at Kerak sent off two car loads of his men by way of the motor track through Mezraa. This party was held at bay by an Israeli detachment detailed for that purpose. Other reinforcements arrived at the top of the scarp on the direct route and were making their way down on foot carrying their weapons and ammunition but they were unlikely to have arrived for several more hours and would have been on the point of exhaustion when they did so.

The assault on the fort was pressed forward with determination and the occupants found themselves being overtaken by the fire of the automatic weapons to which their rifles could only make an inadequate counter; in a couple of hours, everyone in the post was wounded though none of the injuries were serious. What was worse, their supply of ammunition, which had not been intended to cope with an eventuality of that sort, was running low. The sergeant in charge decided, therefore, to withdraw his party into the crags to the east of the building before the post was entirely overrun. Thus, after smashing their wireless set, he and his bandaged and bloodstained followers, filled their bandoliers and pockets with cartridges, picked up full water bottles and some hunks of bread and ran the gauntlet through the bushes for a couple of hundred yards to the first foothills where they took cover behind boulders and reopened fire. They were joined in their new position by several more parties of tribesmen who had been attracted by the noise of the firing, and had left their flocks to be driven further up into the rough country by their women and boys.

While all this was happening, a garbled report of events which considerably magnified the strength of the attacking force, reached the Ministry of the Interior at Amman over the police communications network. The senior official in the office reacted by sending off a series of orders which were so wildly impracticable that no one took any notice of them. The conduct of the war suffered frequently from such interference by senior well meaning and ill-informed persons. A classic example of this occurred when the Amir Naif, the second son of King Abdullah, visited the positions of the artillery which was supporting the front line in Jerusalem and insisted that all the available supplies of ammunition should be moved up to the guns at once. He considered it senseless to move the shells forward in small numbers at regular intervals. Another instance was when a very senior officer of the police section of the Arab Legion flew into a frenzy on finding an ambulance convoy waiting at a roadside rendezvous, while the drivers were snatching a few hours well-earned sleep. He sent the whole lot driving madly towards the front line with the result that all arrangements for the evacuation of sick and wounded men broke down for the day. He asked his victims whether they knew in fact that there was a war in progress.

I was not exempted from the consequences of the alarmist exchanges which were touched off by the episode at Es Safi. In times of special stress, the Jordanians were inclined to forget that both Palestine and Jordan were no longer under British control and I was often pressed to do something about a crisis which was certainly no official business of mine. In the present instance, when Jordanian territory was actually invaded, there were grounds for invoking the terms of the Anglo-Jordan

Treaty of Alliance and this was done repeatedly by excited officials over the telephone. I had difficulty in convincing the callers that there was nothing I could do immediately to preserve the territorial integrity of their country.

In the face of the continued resistance from the men on the hillside and with the prospect of the Arab side being still further reinforced before long, the Israelis decided to break off the action and to withdraw to the potash works to which the few head of cattle which they had captured in the village had already been driven.

The wounded policemen were in no state to follow the retreating party and most of the tribesmen decided that there was no point in pursuit, despite the exhortations of the man who had been beaten up. The latter eventually shouted: 'If you will not help me to take my revenge on those dogs, I will have to do it single handed'. He borrowed a rifle and some cartridges from a friend and slipped away through the bushes. Not long afterwards, the others heard the single crack of his firearm followed by the sound of a ragged volley with which the Israelis retaliated. The sound of the firing became more distant and ceased altogether. The next day, searchers found the body of the revengeful tribesman lying riddled with bullets, several miles to the west of the village.

I was told the tale by a local sheikh who claimed that, as some people combed out the firing positions which had been occupied by the Israelis, one of them had shouted 'Here is one of them'. Then, after a short pause, 'By God, its a girl'. Behind a bush lay the body of a dark-haired girl clad in a khaki shirt and shorts, huddled by the side of a sten gun which she had been firing; she had been killed by a bullet through the chest. She was given a decent burial by the tribesmen whose ideas about the treatment of women, dead or alive, were more civilised than those prevailing in Arab Palestine.

It was curious that the dead girl should be buried in a place where there was a cemetery with tomb stones apparently dating from the fifth or sixth century of our era, bearing painted inscriptions in Hebrew. Judging by the size of the burial ground, there must have been a fair-sized Jewish community living at Es Safi in those days.

Long afterwards, some Israelis told me that the original purpose of the raid had been to secure a supply of fresh meat for the people living at the potash works and that the attack on the police post had been due to an excess of zeal on the part of the Israeli detachment whose orders had been to cover the operations of those rounding up the livestock. I had always believed that the real cause of the affair was the desire of some young men, who were suffering from inactivity and boredom, to play some active part in their country's fight for independence. My tribal friend from Kerak summed up the position quite neatly when he commented 'It was rather a waste of effort by the Jews for the sake of a few miserable cows and goats. The only people on our side who got something for nothing were the policemen who walked down the hill and had to be given a new issue of boots in consequence'. There was some point in the last remark because the tribesmen who had participated in the affair had petitioned for the replacement of the rifle ammunition which they claimed to have expended. Their claims amounted to thousands of rounds, far more than they could possibly have carried on their persons. As a result of their greed, they got nothing.

The Jordanian government considered mounting a punitive expedition against the potash works at Jebel Usdum but their forces were too heavily committed elsewhere and, in the event, the only official reprisal by the Arabs was an abortive raid a few days after the attack by an Anson aircraft of the Iraqi Air Force at Mafraq. The machine scattered a few light anti-personnel bombs around the works without doing any appreciable damage. It was almost the last of the Iraqi aircraft to be in operational condition. Some desultory sniping by the local tribesmen was equally ineffective. The war in the Dead Sea area then ceased for good.

The affair had only been a side show but it had been remarkable because it had been the only fight to take place on Jordanian soil during the 1948–49 hostilities.

Shortly after the Israeli Government came into being, they nationalised the two commercial concessions issued by the Palestine Government to the Palestine Electricity Corporation and the Palestine Potash Corporation. The Jordanian Government took no formal action to annul the Transjordanian concessions given to those firms because they considered that the agreements had lapsed with the termination of the mandate.

CHAPTER 7

War in the Air

The Six Day War of 1967 was decided in favour of the Israelis largely through their predominance in the air, but in the War of Independence the part played by aircraft was of secondary importance.

At the beginning of 1949, the air arm of the Arab Legion was embryonic and consisted of a handful of light transport aircraft such as Doves and Magisters. The absence of fighter planes was a matter for which the Jordanians blamed His Majesty's Government; they held that it placed too great a handicap on the fighting capacity of the Arab Legion. In point of fact, the few fighters possessed by Israel were employed against the more modern machines of the Egyptian Air Force so that the lack of fighters did not make all that much difference to the Jordanians. One of the considerations which affected the issue from the British point of view was the fact that they would have been expected to supply the pilots as well as the aircraft.

Those of us living in Amman, cozened ourselves into believing that the absence of any means of defence against air attack afforded us some sort of immunity from such. An air raid on Damascus by an odd Flying Fortress acquired by Israel, which inflicted some casualties and damage, did not shake our complacent attitude.

Events proved that we were wrong when I was awakened out of a deep sleep one night, about three o'clock in the morning, by the unmistakable noise of the rhythmic crumps of the explosions of a stick of bombs. The sound was not distant and seemed to come from the direction of the railway station near to which were situated both the Arab Legion central depot and the Royal Air Force camp. I jumped out of bed and looked out of my bedroom window, which faced in that direction, to see a most astounding picture. All the lights in the station area were blazing and from the centre of the ring of arc lamps which marked the Royal Air Force camp, there rose four or five columns of smoke from the spots where the bombs had just struck; above, at no great height, I could see the navigation lights of an aircraft, presumably the source of the bombs, which was still circling over its target but which turned, as I watched, towards the town of Amman on a course which would bring it directly over my house.

As the aircraft drew away from the vicinity of the station, the siren of the Royal Air Force began to wail a belated alarm into the night, although I imagine that all the occupants of the camp were already thoroughly alarmed by the unheralded arrival of the missiles from the sky.

It then occurred to me that the Israeli pilot might well have been briefed first to bomb the Arab Legion depot and then to attack the royal palace. The King's quarters consisted of a number of isolated buildings situated on a hill top due west of the railway station. As my house stood just to the east of the Palace grounds, it would be the first house to draw the attention of the pilot and would appear to him to be the first part of the palace complex. It might well be too conspicuous a target for him to ignore. So, I ran along the corridor to my wife's bedroom and called to her to get down the stairs to my study, which had been selected by an air raid precaution expert during the Second World War as the room best fitted to resist the effects of a hit by a bomb. As she got up and huddled into her dressing gown, I went on to bang on the door of the guest room further along the passage which was occupied by Sir Hugh Dow the British Consul General in Jerusalem who had replaced Beaumont. I shouted similar instructions to our guest.

At first, neither my wife or Dow showed any particular haste about doing what I said, but as I could hear the rising hum of the engines of the aircraft as it came towards us, I led the way to the top of the staircase urging the others to make more speed. At the moment we reached the top of the first flight of steps, someone in the power house in the town, doubtless recalling the war time black-out orders, turned off the electric power at the main and plunged the whole of Amman into darkness, thus creating confusion where little had existed before. Few people in the town had realised yet that the place was undergoing the first air raid in its history.

After ten years of residence in the house, I knew my way down the stairs by heart and, as I stood at the bottom and called to the others to hurry, I could hear my wife's voice saying calmly, 'now then, count twelve steps and then turn half to the left and start down another six'. She was leading Dow by the hand; he was completely lost in a strange house without lights and, moreover, was experiencing his first taste of battle. I was always in favour of taking things quietly in a crisis but I felt that they were exaggerating, so I hustled them across the big assembly room to the study. The large room was two storeys high and crowned with a dome with skylights which were particularly vulnerable to attack from the air.

As we passed through the door of the study, we heard the rising scream of the fall of the first bomb which culminated in a terrific crash as it detonated in the garden and blew the glass door which led from the garden into the assembly room. Had we been a second later in reaching the study, we could hardly have escaped injury from the broken glass which was sent flying across the room like shrapnel. As we squatted on the floor of the study, to get below the level of the window, the house was shaken by the explosions of two more bombs which bracketed the building with near misses. The aircraft then passed over the palace itself, which it did not attack, but merely scattered other bombs more or less indiscriminately over the town.

The only riposte to the attack came from the palace, where a young bedouin retainer of the King gave the instinctive reaction of the son of a race of fighters and opened fire on the aircraft with a service rifle. The action was entirely ineffective but it made him, and many others who heard the staccato cracks of the rifle, feel better. As the bombs crashed down amongst the houses of the town, there was a further crackle of rifle fire and pistol shots in reply, punctuated by the shrill blasts of whistles on which all Arab policemen fall back when they are faced with an unexpected emergency.

In all, the Israelis dropped sixteen light anti-personnel bombs and the damage done to buildings was, in consequence, only of a minor nature. But for a piece of rashness on the part of five Arabs who insisted on going out on to the roof of their house to see the fun, and were killed by a random hit on the edge of the parapet, the raid would not have resulted in any loss of life despite all the noise and the smoke. The only other casualty was a calf belonging to a bedouin family who lived just outside the fence of my garden. The animal was killed by the last bomb aimed at my house.

When the aircraft had flown away westward, with its lights still glowing, and the noise from the town had faded away, we decided to go back to bed and try to resume our interrupted sleep, but it was not to be. Shortly after we had retired, the policemen on guard at the gate knocked us up to announce that Broadhurst of the Arab Legion had just arrived to find out if we were all right. He was the only person to show any anxiety about our safety at the time and we considered that it was very remiss on the part of the legation staff who should have been concerned about our well being.

While discussing the event the next day with the King, I remarked jokingly that he owed me a debt of gratitude for having drawn the attack designed for the palace. He smiled and said: 'My debt is to God and so is yours'. It transpired, many months later, that the pilot of the aircraft, which had been a commercial de Havilland Rapide adapted as a light bomber, had, as I thought, been instructed to attack the palace, but who had dropped on my house the quota of missiles which had been intended for use against the true target. The King, incidentally, was aggrieved that his place of abode should have been singled out in this way. He felt that, of all the Arab leaders, he had done least to earn Jewish enmity.

My administrative staff had been having some trouble with the Ministry of Works in London about the maintenance of our quarters, but they were now able to report that my residence, the Second Secretary's house, the chancery and the wireless operators' mess had all been damaged by the bombs. In fact, it was surprising what destruction was attributed to the raid to be made good by a suspicious Ministry of Works who obviously had their doubts but could prove nothing. It was also a coincidence that the raid followed shortly after a guest night at the wireless operators' mess and that it smashed such a lot of glass and crockery.

The fact that so many British installations suffered from the attack caused a certain amount of rather malicious amusement. Like the King, I did not feel that I and my staff had done anything to deserve what had happened to us.

The Royal Air Force had been specially fortunate in escaping without casualties, although taken completely by surprise, like everyone else in Amman. The stick of bombs had fallen right across the tarmac parade ground and their damage had been limited to some holes in adjacent hangars and the small aircraft which they held. How different a story it would have been had the fuel tanks been hit or had the missiles fallen on the flimsy barracks which had been full of sleeping men.

In the course of the ensuing week, light anti-aircraft guns were placed in position around the palace and I was caused a lot of embarrassment when the Transjordanian government demanded the immediate supply of heavier guns and searchlights. Failure to produce these things called forth bitter reproaches and renewed blame for not giving Jordan aircraft of military value. I could find no complete reply to these representations and the suggestion that Jordan could not really afford such luxuries did not seem to give any consolation to the Transjordanians.

Another result of the affair was the reopening in the centre of the city of a number of air raid shelters which had been walled up since the end of the last world war. Once they were open, these structures served, as they had done before, as admirable public latrines. Otherwise, the effect of the raid on the progress of the conflict was virtually nil. That fact must have been realised by the Israeli commanders because attacks of that sort from the air were not renewed.

During the winter months of each year, it had become my almost invariable habit to go down on Saturday afternoons to King Abdullah's winter quarters at Shunet Nimreen in the Jordan Valley and to stay there until the following day. Those visits enabled me to keep in close touch with the King; secondly, they got me away from my office work for a spell and, lastly, they enabled me to get some physical exercise. The exercise came on Sunday when I joined some Arab friends, who owned and farmed lands on the east bank of the river Jordan, and went with them for the day shooting game in the wild country which lay between their holding and the Dead Sea.

The King was getting on in years and was becoming fixed in his ways, so that the programme of the weekly Saturday evenings which we spent together usually followed the same pattern. I arrived at about four o'clock in the afternoon, had tea with the King and talked business until about six o'clock; then there were amusements, attended by the personal staff, which as often as not took the form of innumerable games of chess played with great skill but at a speed far in excess of European standards. The dinner was served at eight o'clock and, afterwards, the King and I sat alone and gossiped for about an hour before retiring to our respective rooms for the night. Luckily for me, we both liked to go to bed early.

One night in the winter of 1948–49, during the truce which preceded the signature at Rhodes of an armistice agreement between Jordan and Israel, we followed the usual evening sequence at Shunet Nimreen and bade each other good night at about ten o'clock. I was reading some official papers in my bed-sitting room when I heard the noise of the engines of a large multi-motored aircraft approaching from over the Dead Sea. This was so unusual an event that I postponed going to bed and stepped out into the garden of the villa which was brilliantly illuminated by electric lights. Outside, I found several of the staff and some guards looking up rather anxiously at the sky and I remarked to the senior aide-de-camp that the compound was too well lit up considering that there was a front line between two hostile armies only a matter of twenty five miles away. He replied, 'Yes I wonder to whom the aircraft belongs. Do you think that we should black out the area?' I answered: 'It is certainly not one of ours and, truce or no truce, we must present a wonderful target if it is an Israeli machine'.

My advice convinced the officer to act without waiting for the King to emerge from his rooms and give orders. He rushed off towards the little generating plant which supplied the electric current, shouting to the mechanic to switch off all the lights immediately. Just as the place was plunged into darkness, King Abdullah came to the doors of his quarters to see what was afoot. He was vexed with the aide-de-camp for having acted without his personal instructions but, at the same time, he could not but agree that the precaution was wise.

There were no air raid shelters in which to take cover,

so we stood and strained our eyes upwards as the throbbing roar approached. We heard whistles blown and orders shouted to a nearby detachment of Iraqi troops whose sentries had also taken alarm. We could still see no sign of the aircraft but, judging by the noise, it seemed to circle round several times over our heads before turning off in a northerly direction up the Jordan Valley. There were some bedouin camps lying out there in which the camp fires still burned and, a few minutes after the aircraft moved away, there was a brilliant flash near one of the camps, followed, a few seconds later, by the thud of the explosion of a heavy bomb. The bomber then passed back over our heads once again, steering in a southerly direction.

The King sent a car to the camps with an officer of the guard to ascertain if anyone had been hurt. The report brought back stated that nobody had been hit but that most of the tribesmen were moving up into the hill without waiting for daylight. They realised that the weather would be colder up there but at least there would be no one throwing bombs about at random. Thus, we congratulated each other on our safety, cursed the Israelis for having disturbed our night's sleep, and returned to our beds.

I followed my usual practice early the next morning and went off with my friends, Mustafa and Mansur al Unsi, to look for game. The King's household came to life before dawn, in time for the early morning prayers, so, there was no difficulty about making an early start. We bucketed off in a jeep, across the shrub, with a picnic lunch in our pockets and we did not get back to my friend's house until about half past three o'clock in the afternoon. On our return, we found their mother in a state of perturbation because there had been a hue and cry for me led by the King in person. According to her account, the King had telephoned several times and had been annoyed when she had only been able to say that she had a vague idea of the direction in which we had gone but had no means of getting into touch with us until we returned home of our own volition.

The King had given no indication of what all the fuss was about but I could only assume that something had gone wrong. I bathed and changed into more respectable clothes before driving back across the plain to Shunet Nimreen. Although King Abdullah was fundamentally kind hearted, he had a peppery temper and he was enraged when I walked into his lounge. He greeted me with the question: 'Where ever have you been all the day? I have had the most unsettling time and there you were, away amusing yourself shooting those miserable little birds and no one could tell me how to find you.' I made soothing noises and pointed out that I had only followed my usual Sunday routine. I assured him that I would have come to him at once had I known that I was wanted and I asked what was wrong. The King went on: 'Fighting has broken out in the Wadi Arabah and Fawzi el Mulki seems to have taken leave of his senses and has restarted the war with Israel without having consulted anyone else beforehand.'

The final straw for the King had been the appearance of an Israeli fighter aircraft soon after the arrival of the news of the clash in the Wadi Arabah. There may well have been some connection between the two events. The fighter had first flown round the neighbourhood of Shunet Nimreen and then followed the main road nearly as far as Amman. Its action had emphasised once again Transjordan's impotence in the air.

The Fawzi el Mulki referred to by the King was the Minister of Defence. He was a native of Damascus who had qualified in England as a member of the Royal College of Veterinary Surgeons with the aid of a grant made by His Majesty's Government. The idea behind the financial aid had been to train a young Arab in a profession which would have been of practical value to the country, but as soon as Fawzi had graduated, he had announced that he was going in for a political career, as though there were not already far too many politicians at large in Jordan. He had adopted an ultra-nationalistic platform and had risen rapidly to the top. The King had made him Minister of Defence with the special task, as I happened to know, of ensuring that the British officers serving in the Arab Legion did not betray the Arab cause. It should be said to his credit that he was of considerable assistance to Glubb when he might easily have been a nuisance.

The trouble in the Wadi Arabah which had upset the King had not been very serious. Possibly through inadvertence, the Israeli convoys to and from Eilat had used a track which might have crossed the Jordanian frontier, and had clashed with an Arab Legion patrol. The boundary in that vicinity had never been demarcated on the ground and it would have been easy for anybody to make an error. The King's instinct had been right not to want the incident magnified into something which could restart a war which had been stopped.

There was a mystery which has never been solved about the heavy bomber from over the Dead Sea. A large fragment of the tail piece of the bombs which had been dropped, had been recovered and it had been found to bear a crudely written inscription in Arabic. The painted writing was in doggrel verse and can be roughly translated as: 'Oh Shertock, you man without nation or honour, we send you this caramel'. Shertock being the original name of Mr Sharrett who became the first Israeli Minister for Foreign Affairs.

Both the Israelis and the Egyptians stoutly maintained that none of their aircraft were in the vicinity of the Dead Sea on the night in question but both the King and I were convinced that the aircraft was Egyptian. The King argued that no one but an Egyptian would go to the trouble of painting nonsense of that type on an aeroplane bomb. What the King did not understand was why a missile addressed to the Israeli Foreign Minister should be dropped near to his winter quarters during a truce. The Egyptians might be ill-informed but hardly to the point of thinking that the Jericho area was in Israeli hands.

I have never been able to suggest a rational explanation of what the affair meant. Perhaps I should be consoled by the fact that by normal standards so many Egyptian actions are irrational.

I caused much amusement at a palace luncheon party later, by remarking that I could not understand why no one had blamed the British for the incident. During the same meal, some reference to the White House made me inquire, in all innocence, why the building was given that name. To the apparent delight of most of those present, my United States colleague explained that the house had been painted white to conceal the traces of the time when it had been set on fire by British troops.

When I finally got back to my home in Amman late on Sunday evening, I received another rebuke–this time from my wife–for going off without saying where I could be found. My wife's afternoon rest had been ruined by repeated telephone calls from people enquiring as to my whereabouts. I resisted the urge to tell her, and other protesters, that the whole object of the Sunday excursions was to go somewhere where I could not be found.

CHAPTER 8

Armistice

By Spring 1949, the leaders of the Arab states which were actively involved in the fighting had had enough of the war. There must have been a sigh of relief in their ranks when, after a final battle around the Gaza Strip, the Egyptian Government signed a preliminary ceasefire and an armistice proper which was signed at Rhodes on February 24th 1949.

The last clash of the Egyptian front took the Israeli forces as far west as the vicinity of El Arish and gave rise to a short crisis during which many people in Israel believed that Great Britain was on the point of entering the war on the side of the Arabs. Perhaps the most interesting fact about the episode was that I and other heads of mission at Beirut and Damascus were not told about it by the Foreign Office.

The Egyptians were the most vocal of the Arab countries involved and, once they had acknowledged defeat, it was a foregone conclusion that the other Arab states would follow suit. The machinery prescribed for disengagement was the same in each case. The establishment of a ceasefire prior to the negotiating of a more permanent arrangement on the neutral territory of Rhodes and under the chairmanship of Dr Bunche, the Mediator of the United Nations Organisation. Each Arab state, with one exception, entered into separate agreement with Israel and the selfish manner in which they all looked to their own interests seemed to indicate that the cause for which they fought was no longer common.

When their turn came, the Jordanian delegation was made up entirely of Arab officers of the Legion in order to forestall further accusations of British treachery. The delegates arrived in Rhodes willing, if not anxious, to sign the preliminary ceasefire accord but they discovered that there were two snags in the way of immediate progress. The first was the procrastination of the Israelis who eventually divulged that they wanted the extreme southern part of the Negev which was still held by a small detachment of the Arab Legion. The Israelis pointed out that the whole of the Negev had been assigned to them under the terms of the partition scheme and they added that they intended to take what was theirs by right, ceasefire or no ceasefire.

The second difficulty was one created by the action of the Iraqi government who, for purposes of internal politics, announced that they had no intention of signing any agreement with Israel and simply proposed to withdraw their troops forthwith, regardless of what everybody else did. The motive behind the Iraqi stand was that of being able to boast, in the future, that they alone of all the Arab states had been strong enough to refuse to sit down and negotiate with the enemy.

At this point, the anxiety of King Abdullah overcame his pride and his discretion and he sent a personal emissary to the Israeli leaders, against the advice of his Prime Minister and myself. We represented to him that, as he had been unable to secure any worthwhile concessions from the Israelis when the outcome of the conflict was still an open question, he was unlikely to do any better now that they had the upper hand. To his retort that there was no harm in trying, we pointed out that he would damage his reputation in the Arab world still further, if, as seemed likely, the move became known. He remained unshaken and insisted on sending a member of his personal staff across the lines.

The Israeli reply was not helpful. They made their agreement to the Arab Legion taking over the Iraqi positions subject to the surrender on that part of the front line of a strip of rich cultivable land covering a superficial area of some four hundred square kilometres. They threatened an all out assault if the take-over was made without their consent. There were less than two thousand Jordanian troops available to replace the ten thousand Iraqi soldiers and, as the latter had no intention of fighting any more, the Jordanian government had no choice but to accept the Israeli terms.

The new and uncompromising attitude adopted by the Israeli leaders towards King Abdullah, now that they were winning the war, reminded me of something which Dr Chaim Weizmann had said in January of 1945 – the last time I had met him. He had invited me to spend a night at his residence in Rehovot in order to talk over the general situation informally. He had given up active political work for the time being and was living in semi-retirement but his guidance was still sought by many of his erstwhile colleagues. He had been one of the Zionist leaders for whom I had had a deep respect and I had accepted his invitation with pleasure after I had obtained the consent of the High Commissioner, Sir Harold MacMichael. (When I had consulted the latter, he had raised his eyebrows but had not objected.)

The house was part of the Institute for Scientific Research which bore Dr Weizmann's name. It was heavily guarded, 'not against Arabs' as he said and, apart from a servant, my host and I were the only occupants. We sat after dinner and talked far into the night about the past and the future. Amongst the points which were touched upon was the practicability of a bi-national state, covering both sides of the Jordan river, on the lines which had been advocated so often by King Abdullah. Dr Weizmann thought that some such scheme might be workable in the future, once a Jewish state had been founded securely. Then he had added the words: 'But your King Abdullah will never sit upon the throne of David'. (I had mentioned that I was working for the elevation of Abdullah to royal dignity.)

To return to the beginning of 1949, signs of future events came in the form of a reference by an Israeli radio commentator to the importance of Israel having an outlet at the gulf of Aqaba. As Jordan's only means of direct access to the world outside, the possession of Aqaba was essential to that country also. In alarm, the Jordanians invoked the terms of the Anglo-Jordanian Treaty of Alliance which entitled them to British protection from attacks on territory belonging to Jordan proper. In response a battalion of British infantry was sent to the port where they were joined by a frigate of the Royal Navy. I flew down to Aqaba to put the ship's commander in the picture and to ensure that he, and the officer commanding the troops, were not too bellicose in their attitudes.

The Israeli assault started on March 7th and the Arab Legion detachment in the Negev was attacked by a superior force. By the end of the month, the Israelis had reached the shore of the Gulf of Aqaba and the whole of the Negev was in their hands. This gave Israel the door to the east which was needed and no attempt was made to cross into Jordanian territory at Aqaba which was still occupied by a British contingent. This last Israeli advance was in defiance of the terms of the ceasefire agreement but appeals by Jordan to the United Nations Organisation were, as usual, disregarded.

The first Israeli reaction to the arrival of the British troops was to send an officer over to propose that a friendly football match should be organised between the two contingents. When that advance was politely rebuffed the Israelis retaliated by kidnapping a British border patrol and holding the sergeant for a week for interrogation. After that episode, the two sides observed each other from a distance.

The Jordanian authorities probably found this period of hostilities the most frustrating. They were learning the hard way that it is more difficult to get out of a war than it is to get into one, especially when one is at the losing end and is abandoned by one's friends and allies. Jordan had lost the game and now the forfeits had to be paid. When the Israelis refused to improve their conditions, King Abdullah appealed to His Majesty's government for support and also sought help from the government of the United States of America. Both administrations made unconvincing excuses for failing to intervene.

Having secured possession of the territory which they wanted, the Israelis signed the armistice agreement with Jordan on April 3rd. In the meanwhile, the Lebanese government had obtained its own armistice on March 23rd. The Iraqis kept to their intention and went back home without signing an agreement, regardless of the harm which they were inflicting on their allies. The Syrians, on the other hand, were in the throes of a revolution, in which I was inadvertently to become involved, and they were too preoccupied with each other to be bothered about peacemaking.

The agreements were supposed to be temporary arrangements pending the negotiation of a peace settlement but, in fact the demarcation line which they defined became the international boundary between Israel and the Arab states for the next twenty years until the war of 1967 put the whole issue back into the melting pot.

About the middle of March, I had been summoned to London by the Foreign Office to discuss a variety of problems concerning the future. The principal topic was to find ways and means of restoring relations with Jordan to their pre-war cordiality. We had not got far with our deliberations when an officer of the Syrian army, named Husni el Zaim, staged a successful *coup-d'état* in Damascus and took over power. This upset came at a most delicate time in Middle Eastern affairs and there was anxiety in the Foreign Office about the effect which it might have on Jordan where opposition elements were trying to create trouble. There was also the probability that King Abdullah would try to further his aims in Syria whilst conditions there were confused. I was told, therefore, to forget about the outstanding items on the agenda and to get back to my post as soon as possible.

It was unfortunate that the earliest flight available was scheduled to land at Damascus and Broadmead, the British Minister there, did not consider it advisable for me to pass through Syrian territory. I was, apparently, too closely identified with the King in the eyes of the Syrian authorities to be welcome there. The Foreign Office arranged, or thought that they had arranged, for the British Overseas Airways aircraft on which my passage was booked, to make a special stop at Cyprus where I would change over to a transport aircraft of the Royal Air Force which would take me straight to Amman.

I did not consider it necessary to mention the proposed landing in Cyprus to any one at Heathrow airport or to the crew of the machine until we were over the island and should have been preparing to descend. It then transpired that the crew knew nothing about an unscheduled stop and could not make one on the spur of the moment. So, I was carried on to Damascus willy-nilly, arriving there about six o'clock in the morning. I was the only passenger to disembark and there was not, of course, any one there to meet me at the airport from the Legation. It was assumed that I had got off in Cyprus.

The airport staff told me that there was a curfew in force and that everyone needed a special pass to be allowed on the streets. I was about to ask them to telephone to Broadmead's residence, when a voice behind me said in Arabic, 'Good God, what are you doing here?' The speaker was a car driver employed by the Iraq Petroleum Company whom I had known at Amman. Apparently, he had come to the airport to meet a company employee who had, wisely, decided to postpone his journey. When

I explained my predicament, the driver offered to take me to the residency using the curfew pass which he carried for himself and the missing passenger. His offer confirmed my theory that some of the most useful friends a man can have are policemen and taxi drivers.

The road blocks in the streets outside were manned by soldiers who appeared to be more than half asleep after being up all the night, and, we drove through without any of them showing any great interest in us. Every time, we passed a patrolling tank, we beamed and waved our hands. The troops looked startled and waved back. Broadmead answered my ring at the front door of his house wearing a dressing gown and he nearly had a fit when he saw who the early caller was. He was very angry that his advice had been ignored and seemed inclined to vent his spleen on me. I retorted that it was no good being angry with me, I had had no desire to see him or his revolution, but fate had brought me to his door and he must now give me breakfast and provide me with transportation to Amman. He did both these things and I was even able to speak to my wife on the telephone and assure people at Amman that I had not gone permanently astray. The frontier at Deraa was closed to travellers and motor traffic but it was possible for me to drive up to one side of the line in Broadmead's car, step across the invisible boundary, while the sentries looked the other way, and then drive off in my own vehicle which had come from Amman to meet me.

As we had anticipated, the *coup d'état* in Syria sparked off a resumption of King Abdullah's futile efforts to further the emergence of a Greater Syria under his rule. There was still no chance of Syria becoming a monarchy but the King found no difficulty in placing bribes in the hands of people who, in return, sent him periodical petitions and telegrams declaring their unswerving devotion to the furthering of his noble intentions.

One of my tasks in London had been to seek to arrange for some additional aid to be given to the refugees in

Jordan. The needs of those unfortunate people were far in excess of the means of the Jordanian government and of the local charitable organisations available for relief purposes and it was obvious that nothing short of an international institution could command the vast sums of money which were going to be required. The United Nations Organisation was in the process of creating the necessary machinery to deal with the situation which had arisen but immediate help was imperative. I represented that it was highly desirable that something should be done by Great Britain independently to restore, to some extent, the damage which we had done to our political image in the Middle East. I met representatives of the British Red Cross and the Order of St. John of Jerusalem while I was in London, with the blessing of the Foreign Office, and they rose to the occasion admirably. A British team of relief workers was sent to Jordan in a surprisingly short time but they did not win many signs of gratitude from the beneficiaries. The refugees believed with some justification, that the British and American governments were partly responsible for their woes and that any aid which came from those quarters was only part payment of a moral debt.

The British Red Cross Society never knew that they provided a Duchess and a White Rabbit for the cast of my Alice-in-Wonderland fantasy which did so much to preserve my sanity. The former was their Chairman, the Duchess of Marlborough, and the latter was a small man with white hair and a pink nose who once said to me, when told that something that he wanted could not be done, 'Oh dear, the Duchess will be annoyed'.

Whilst working in London, I shared a room at the over-crowded Foreign Office with Knox Helm who was the British Minister designate in Tel Aviv. Allowing for the fact that he was in the more comfortable position of not being emotionally involved in the problem in any way, we held similar views as how best to tackle the wide field of problems which faced our two missions. Some of our differences of approach arose from the fact that he was a career diplomat while I had entered the Foreign Service almost by accident.

The conclusion of the armistice enabled affairs to return to something approaching normalcy. The most important and urgent matter for my attention was the restoration of my personal relations with King Abdullah to their previously cordial footing. We had been friends since the time I had met him on his first arrival in Jordan in March 1921. One cannot explain the instinctive liking between individuals such as existed in our case, but the reason why the feeling lasted for thirty years was probably due to the fact that I always gave him an honest opinion on any matter under consideration. He did not always agree with my opinion and he was sometimes irritated by what I said but, at least, he was sure that what I recommended was what I believed to be for the best.

This frankness did not mean that I could ever take anything for granted as far as the King was concerned or that I could speak to him bluntly if we disagreed. He was touchy and expected to receive the courtesy which he extended to others. He preferred negative responses to be delivered in private but, if that was impossible, I knew how to appear to agree with him in a manner which he knew really implied dissent.

Over the years, we developed what amounted to a secret talking code. For instance, if I said, 'His Majesty's Government hopes that your Majesty will accept this advice'; it meant that I did not agree with what was recommended and that I would support him if he resisted. But, if I used the form 'and I hope that you will accept', it meant that I did agree with the advice and that it had better be taken.

He was quick on the uptake and, once in the days of the mandate, when he was proposing some unacceptable financial racket, he stopped his exposition and said: 'I suppose that it is no good my going on?' I answered 'but I have not said anything'. He went on: 'I know that but you did this'. He then shifted in his seat in a mannerism which I realised, for the first time, I use when I have decided to disagree with someone.

I knew that he used my name frequently without my knowledge, to throw the odium for some unpopular decision or refusal on to somebody else but that was the price which any *éminence grise* must pay for his, or her, influence.

On the official side, the embargo on the issue of funds and military supplies was lifted, arrears of payments due under the terms of the Anglo-Jordanian Treaty were paid up to date and the stock of ammunition of the Arab Legion was restored to its pre-war level. Taking into account the peril into which they had been placed by our action, the Jordanians were more forgiving than we had any right to expect. Forgiveness, however, did not mean that our actions were forgotten.

His Majesty's Government also gave formal recognition to the annexation of the West Bank by Jordan, which they had already accepted *de facto*. They included, however, a proviso on the subject of Jerusalem because that city was still the subject of a United Nations resolution to the effect that it should be internationalised. The fact that neither the Israelis or the Arabs took any notice of the resolution, did not discourage the British Government from bending over backwards in its anxiety to avoid doing anything which might be taken as disregard of its terms. In pursuance of this policy, Helm and his Chancery stayed in Tel Aviv when the Israeli Government moved its seat to Jerusalem. For the same reason, while the west bank became part of my parish, Arab Jerusalem continued to be excluded and the Consul General there continued to function in a vacuum.

Tewfiq abul Huda and his fellow ministers in the cabinet resigned from sheer exhaustion and they were replaced by a new government headed by another native of Palestine, Samir Rifai. For the first time, half the members of the new Ministry came from the west bank. The new appointments did not indicate any change of policy and both the teams from the west and the east were supporters of the monarchy.

In the general process of clearing up the mess, the consular section of my legation was obliged to deal with the men who had deserted during the last days of the mandate, either from the British Land Forces, the Royal Air Force or the British Section of the Palestine Police and had joined the ranks of one of the irregular formations of Arab fighters. There were a surprising number of these absentees and it was alleged that, at one time, the section of the Fighters which was controlled by the political opponents of the Mufti, had included a British platoon with an armoured police car. There was no truth in reports that British deserters were enlisted in the Arab Legion. Unit commanders of the Legion had orders not to have any truck with deserters.

The end of the fighting had left these people without employment or income and they wanted to get home. When questioned about their motives in taking up arms for the Arab cause, most of these men claimed to have been inspired by the love of adventure. This may have been true in some cases but I suspected that there had been other reasons too. Some had been talked into it by Arab girl friends, others may have been motivated by racial bias but it was certain that financial gain cannot have influenced many of them. The pay was poor and fell into arrears which were never settled but the living conditions were the worst part of the bargain. An ex-private of the British Army could not be expected to approve of the daily ration of Arab bread and raw onions with very little else. In the event the British volunteers were not of great military value to their employers and they were frequently unmitigated nuisances regarding the conditions of service.

As soon as the Arab irregular units broke up, most of their British personnel hitch-hiked their way to Amman and came to my door demanding repatriation. Those who

had deserted from one of the armed services were put under
arrest by the Provost Marshal of the Royal Air Force
and flown to the United Kingdom to be court-martialled.
The ex-policemen were more difficult to dispose of, some
of them had lost their papers and some had destroyed
them; another complication was that they had not committed a breach of the laws of Jordan or Great Britain
and no legal proceedings could be instituted against them
in those countries. The Palestine Government, which they
offended, had ceased to exist. In the end, we decided to
treat them as distressed British subjects and to send them
home without further ado.

Notwithstanding the exclusion of Jerusalem from my
jurisdiction, I became involved in two questions concerning that city. One of the Israeli enclaves left in the Arab
part of Jerusalem at the end of the first phase of the
fighting there, had been the Hebrew University and the
Hadassah Hospital on the Mount of Olives. When the
Arab Legion prepared to reduce that position, it was represented to the Jordanians that an attack on such buildings
on the holy mountain would alienate public opinion in
the United States of America. The Arab Legion consented,
therefore to an arrangement made by Count Bernadotte
for the two institutes to be demilitarised and handed over
to the custody of the United Nations Organisation; pending completion of the transfer, a party of Israeli police
were to be left in the buildings to protect them from
looters. The police guards were to be kept supplied by
periodical convoys. Before United Nations personnel
could take over from the police, Count Bernadotte was
assassinated. Some time after that event, the police guard
changed, in some mysterious manner, into a company
of Israeli infantry which was still in position when the
armistice was signed.

One of the defensive posts of the Hadassah Hospital
stood on the perimeter wall of the adjacent British War
Cemetery and the Arab Legion had a corresponding post
at the other end of the burial ground. When the dust

of the combat had settled, the Imperial War Graves Commission sought permission to resume possession of its property and to repair the damage done to the graves during the fighting. Both the sides said that they had no objection to the commission taking charge of the cemetery, but they added that any maintenance work would have to be done under the supervision of their troops. This proviso sounded reasonable but, in practice, it meant that nothing could be done; the Arabs would not let the Israelis exercise authority and the latter would not accept the Arabs. Helm in Tel Aviv could not shift the Israelis from their stand and I was equally unsuccessful with the Jordanians. Soldiers lay unattended on the Mount of Olives as did occupants of the old Jewish graveyards further down the hill in the valley of Gethsemane. My sister-in-law, Zoe Kirkbride, rested in the Protestant Cemetery on Mount Zion, which was in no man's land also. My mother's grave was in Bethlehem a few hundred yards on the Jordanian side of the armistice line.

The second question arose from the fact that I was still an *ex-officio* and founder member of the board of trustees of the Palestine Archeological Museum of Jerusalem. That body had never met and the Foreign Office expected me to assemble its members so that they could take charge of the institution.

The Museum was housed in a building which was, in my opinion, the best of the many attractive architectural works which Austen Harrison had designed in Palestine; the collection of choice antiquities was of unique interest to students of the History of the Holy Land and included many items of high intrinsic value. The principal credit for the survival of the museum and its contents intact after the fighting inside the city, was due to a Mr Joseph Saad, who had been its clerk during the mandatory period and who had taken over control of his own initiative, when the British officials had left Palestine. He had rallied the Arab attendants who had had their appointments terminated by the out-going government and he had induced them to return to their duties and protect the place from the attentions of the looters which disorder always brings in its train. He and his men had worked for a period of nearly six months without knowing who would pay them.

Assisted by Gerald Harding, who was the Curator of Antiquities of the Jordanian Government, I got into touch with the nominated members of the board who were available locally and invited them to meet informally at my house in Amman for tea and there to organise an inaugural meeting of the board at a later date in the Museum. When the board assembled the representative of the Jordanian Government, the Director of the American School of Oriental Research, the Director of the Dominican Fathers Biblical College of St. Stephen and a Monsieur Seyrig from Beirut and I were present. As a matter of form, an invitation was sent through Cyprus to Mr Sukenik, Archeological Professor of the Hebrew University, but, naturally, he could not manage to attend in the circumstances.

We formally assumed control of the Museum and of its finances which consisted of an endowment which brought in a sum of about nine thousand pounds a year. We elected Father de Vaux of the Dominicans as our chairman, Gerald was made Secretary of the institution in an honorary capacity and Mr Saad and his attendants were confirmed in their posts with arrears of pay as from May 15th. The Museum was reopened to the public a few weeks later.

Possibly in an unconscious effort to escape from the current disasters of this world, I was a devoted, albeit amateurish, archeologist and numismatist and, as such, I got great pleasure in spending the little time I had to spare on the affairs of the Museum. It was, incidentally, very convenient for me to have a legitimate excuse for visiting Jerusalem. One exhibit in the Museum had a special attraction for me, it was the body of a Neanderthal woman, embedded, in fossilised form, in a block of limestone which had been found in a cave on Mount Carmel. She lay on her side with her knees slightly bent and only the top layer of her stone shroud was chipped away from her remains. Her humanity was proved in a poignant manner by the necklace of coloured pebbles which encircled her neck and the fillet of shells which adorned her forehead. She was said to have lived nearly thirty thousand years ago and, in times of stress, I found consolation in the contemplation of her great age. Somehow, the span of time seemed to reduce the proportions of our current troubles.

I had to resign from the board on leaving for Libya and I was pained to see from afar what I considered to be the failure of my successors in their duty to safeguard the international character of the institution, which was left in their charge. On the excuse that the annual revenue from the endowment and from fees charged for admission, was insufficient for the proper maintenance of the Museum, the trustees made over the place and its contents to the Jordanian Government. I am sure that it might have been possible to raise the funds needed to preserve its independence as an international institution.

In 1967, the Museum fell, together with the whole of the west bank, into the hands of the Israelis.

CHAPTER 9

Incidents

The collapse of all their dreams and hopes, left the Palestinian Arabs in a bitter mood and in no mind to accept the conclusion of an armistice agreement once they had lost their chance of recovering possession of their homeland. It was only natural for them to seek to blame others for their own failures and mistakes and the readiest scapegoats were the King, Glubb and the Arab Legion, and the British and American Governments whose past policies had enabled the Jewish immigrants to establish themselves in the first place aroused much hatred. The signing of the agreement removed the fear of losing more land to the Israelis but it did not bring anything like peace to the boundary line which now divided Palestine. As one bedouin sheikh wittily remarked to me, 'The only difference is that it used to be illegal to shoot during the truces; now it is always illegal to shoot and everybody continues to do so.'

There ensued an apparently endless series of frontier incidents, most of which were concerned with persons referred to in the official reports as infiltrators. Any stranger reading those reports would probably have come to the conclusion that infiltrators were criminals of the worst type but, in fact, most of them were people who were either trying to get back to their homes in Israel or, having been there, were trying to get across to Jordan. There was a minority of real Arab predators who were out to kill and rob the usurpers.

The Jordanian authorities did their best to check clandestine crossing of the frontier, not because they liked the Israelis, but because they could not afford to risk a bilateral resumption of the war now that they had been virtually abandoned by their Arab allies. Short of stationing a sentry at gaps of only a few yards, there was no way, however, of stopping all movement across such a long and complex boundary which was not demarcated on the ground. The refugees in Jordan, whose number had increased to half a million, could not understand the apparent desire of the Arab Legion to assist their enemies in restricting freedom of movement and their bitterness towards their hosts grew accordingly.

The Israeli response to the infiltrators took the form of raids by detachments of their forces over the frontier and the indiscriminate shooting of the unfortunates whose homes happened to be nearest to the boundary. There was no doubt that living in the vicinity was the only offence of many of the victims of these incursions. The number of Jordanian troops available to protect villagers was inadequate, so, after there had been one hundred and seventeen Israeli raids of reprisal between December 1949 and October 1950, the Jordanian Government decided to issue a number of rifles to the inhabitants of the exposed areas and to send non-commissioned officers to train selected young men in the use of these arms.

This distribution of arms did a lot to correct the unpopularity of the Jordanian Government which had been engendered by the flood of propaganda which had been put out against it by the information media of Egypt and Syria. The headman of one frontier village said to me, 'We could not believe our eyes when the rifles were given to us free of charge. The notables in the cities have twice collected money from us with which to buy us weapons but the arms never came.' I encouraged Glubb and the Jordanian Ministers to do their utmost to win the active co-operation of the Palestinian peasants in all the activities of government.

The change of sentiment amongst the villagers towards the Arab Legion made it possible to extend to Palestine a new organisation called the National Guard which was being recruited at first on the east bank. A law was enacted under the terms of which all male Jordanians of a certain age were liable to undergo a month's military training per year and to be available for the defence of their homes at all times. The men accepted as members of the National Guard were given uniforms and arms, but were not paid. The new force came under the administrative and operational control of the local commander of the Arab Legion. The appearance of what amounted to a second line to the regular army resulted in there being a marked diminution in the number of raids across the frontier.

During the same ten months as those referred to above, seventy-six intrusions by Israeli aircraft into Jordanian air space were reported to the Truce Commission. One of these incidents concerned the commercial air service which was operated from Amman by the Arab Airways Association between Amman and Beirut. The custom had grown, since the conclusion of the armistice, for those aircraft to take a short cut across Israeli territory, between the Lebanon and Jordan. Technically this crossing of Upper Galilee was in breach of the armistice but no one objected until the afternoon in question, when the crimson coloured Rapide took off from the airport of Beirut piloted by a British captain and with a passenger list which included two British journalists—John Nixon and David Woodford. There were also an American and three Jordanian businessmen aboard.

The aircraft followed its usual route but, just before it crossed over the river Jordan, into its home territory, an Israeli fighter aircraft dived past the Rapide's nose lowering and raising its flaps as it did so. During the subsequent enquiry which was held under the auspices of the United Nations Truce Commission, the Israeli pilot explained that he had intended his move to be a signal to the other pilot to land at the nearest Israeli airfield. The captain of the Rapide realised that he was being told to descend but, as he was over Jordanian territory, he disregarded the manoeuvre and its repetitions and held to his course while gradually losing altitude. The Israeli machine then dived past once more but, this time, firing its cannon as a final warning; the Rapide's pilot responded by putting his machine into a steeper dive with the intention of making an emergency landing on the first flat piece of ground. The fighter wheeled away, gained height and then attacked in grim earnest the next time it dived. it scored several direct hits on the rear part of the Rapide; missing all the passengers, but setting the aeroplane alight.

The cabin of the stricken machine rapidly filled with smoke and, as it was evident that it would only be a matter of seconds before there was a general conflagration, the pilot went into a nose dive as his opponent came back showing every intention of attacking him again. The Rapide flattened out at a height of thirty or forty feet above a stony field in preparation for a crash landing. The pursuer roared past overhead once more but without firing, probably because the ground was too close to enable his aircraft to depress its nose sufficiently without its being in danger of hitting the earth.

By this time, the passengers in the Rapide were getting desperate and they crowded behind the pilot's seat to avoid the flames, then suddenly Nixon shouted to Woodford to follow him and staggered through the smoke to the door which he jerked open and jumped through, followed closely by his companion. When the pilot realised what had happened, he yelled to the remaining occupants to stay where they were and to hold on tight; he then brought the machine down on to the ground. The wheels carried the aircraft for about twenty yards before both tyres were punctured by sharp stones and the undercarriage collapsed bringing the Rapide to a stop resting on the fuselage. The rear of the cabin was a mass of flames and its occupants were already singed, so, the pilot smashed the windscreen in front of his seat and forced his way through the aperture followed by the rest who fought amongst themselves to get out. They all rolled out on to the ground, bruised, cut, and burnt, but still alive. Almost immediately the wreck was evacuated, the flames reached the fuel tanks and it exploded into a furnace of red fire crowned by billowing black smoke. The Israeli fighter, which was all of nine miles inside Jordanian territory by now, flew off to the westward.

Men hastened up from a nearby village to offer help to the survivors but Nixon and Woodford were found to be past the need for human assistance. Their fall from a height of at least thirty feet, from an aircraft which was travelling at about one hundred and fifty miles an hour could not have failed to have fatal consequences. Both men seemed to have most of their bones broken, including their necks, and their deaths must have been instantaneous.

We buried the remains of the two dead men the next day on the dreary hillside which serves as a cemetery for the various Christian communities at Amman. There is little soil there and each grave had to be hacked out of the solid but friable rock. A volunteer bearing party was provided by men from the Royal Air Force camp and those who followed the coffins up the rugged track, which was too rough and narrow to be used by motor transport, included Gerald Harding and myself. We were the only friends of the deceased who were present. The rest of the group were made up of the pilot of the Rapide, whose singed neck and forearms were swathed in bandages, the Reverend Blackburn, who was the local leader of the Church Missionary Society, and a number of inquisitive Arabs, both grown up and otherwise, who had joined themselves to the little procession at the bottom of the hill.

The coffins had been knocked together in haste by a

local carpenter and they were crude bits of work by any standard. In order to conceal their defects, they were both covered over with a material which was not usually associated with funerals. As we toiled up the path towards the graves, Gerald turned his face to me and said, 'Do you know, Kirk? I am sure that David must be amused that his coffin should be covered with pink tulle'.

There was a strong wind blowing across the hill as we stood round the two shallow trenches opened in the rock. Blackburn, with his clerical robes fluttering, read through the burial service against a background of loud comment from the Arab spectators who squatted on neighbouring tombs, until a stray Arab Legionary, who had drifted up, turned on the chorus and shouted in Arabic, 'Shut up. Cannot you see that these people are praying?' There were no further interruptions after that intervention.

As I turned away from the desolate place, with a feeling of futility which nearly always overtakes me on such occasions, two thoughts were uppermost in my mind. Firstly, 'What a waste, they need not have jumped.' Secondly, 'What an awful hole in which to have one's last resting place.'

I could not quite follow the process of reasoning which brought His Majesty's Government to the conclusion that the Jordanian Government was morally bound to pay compensation to the dependants of Nixon and Woodford. The Jordanians could not comprehend why they should have been penalised for having had an aircraft shot down over their own territory but, eventually, they paid up to avoid further arguments. They were probably influenced by the fact that the ultimate source of the money was, in any event, Great Britain.

Another Rapide aircraft belonging to the same company, which was flying over the Negev on its way to Egypt, was subsequently forced down into Israel. The occupants were released almost immediately but the machine was impounded. After this second incident, all Jordanian aircraft avoided flying over Israeli air space.

One might have expected Jerusalem, which was bisected by the armistice line, to be at the centre of the most frequent incidents, but, paradoxically, it was one of the quietest sectors of the boundary. The explanation lay in the fact that the two parts of the city were divided by a strip of no-man's-land, from Mount Zion to the south of Mount Scopus. The barrier was a sore sight for those who had known the city in its happier days; the strip consisted of a stretch of ruined houses flanked, on the Jordanian side, by the old Turkish walls for part of the distance, then by a new wall running from the Damascus gate to the foot of Mount Scopus. On the Israeli side, the barrier was bordered by a barbed wire fence which linked up with fortified buildings. At first, there was no crossing place but, in time, a villa owned by a Mr Mandelbaum was converted into a gate and was named after its owner.

King Abdullah was specially sensitive to the gloom in Jerusalem and to the ugliness of the neutral zone but he felt it to be wise to woo his new, and sometimes reluctant, subjects by living in their midst for part of the time. His first place of lodging was in a refurbished apartment in the Haram es Sherif enclosure but he complained that the ancient environment depressed him. His feeling may have been a presentiment of death because his windows overlooked the mosque in which he was to be assassinated a few years later. He was moved next to a modern house standing on the lower slope of Mount Scopus and only a few yards from the edge of no-man's-land, so that he had a clear view into Israel. He professed to be deeply offended in his dignity when he discovered that the oddly dressed people who stared at him, as he sat on a balcony, from the other side of the barbed wire fence, were Jews. He moved back to the Haram es Sherif where he was only likely to see Moslems with an occasional Christian tourist.

Whilst the King could object, in public, to the presence of Israelis too close to his house in Jerusalem, he was quite ready, when it suited him, to receive their official representatives at his residence at Shunet Nimreen, east of the Jordan river. He was instrumental in arranging a series of more or less secret talks during the autumn of 1949, between the Prime Minister of Jordan, Samir Rifai, and a senior official of the Israeli Ministry for Foreign Affairs, named Shiloah. I had known Shiloah quite well, under his original name of Zaslani, when I had been the District Commissioner for Galilee and Acre in the years 1937–39. The visitor used to travel down from Jerusalem in a car sent by the King, dine at the royal table with the Prime Minister and then retire with the latter to an ante-chamber for discussions which seemed to be interminable. King Abdullah used to stay up for as long as he could keep his eyes open in the hope that some positive result might emerge. The exchange usually terminated at about three o'clock on the morning after which Shiloah went back across the lines. I marvelled at the amount of time the two participants managed to take up with their discussions.

The King made no secret of the fact that his objective was to salvage some of the territory which the Arabs had lost in the débacle. The Israelis appeared to join in the debates with the aim of making a separate peace settlement with Jordan and so breaking the Arab boycott which was in the process of being formed. The main plank of the Jordanian argument was that they could only follow a policy contrary to that of the other Arab countries if, by so doing, they recovered sufficient Arab land to justify their action in the eyes of the Palestinians and to silence the attacks of their many enemies. The difficulty was that the Israeli Government was not ready to restore any meaningful area of land important enough to enable the King and his followers to defy hostile Arab opinion and come to terms.

The main demand made by Samir Rifai was free access to the coast of the Mediterranean Sea and he pressed hard for the transfer to Jordan of a wide strip of land connecting Jordan with the ancient port of Ascalon which was known to the Arabs as Mejdel. Shiloah ruled out any territorial adjustment which would separate the Negev from the rest of Israel; he added, moreover, that his government had special plans in hand for the port of Mejdel. He offered instead technical advice and aid plus a transit agreement and a free zone in a Mediterranean port for Jordanian imports and exports. Samir Rifai countered, with some justification, that the last two points would favour the Israeli economy almost as much as that of Jordan. The Jordanian request that the Israeli Government should relieve the crushing economic burden imposed on Jordan by the presence of a huge number of refugees was also fruitless. Shiloah refused to consider the return to their homes of any large number of refugees except as part of a general peace settlement with all the belligerent Arab countries.

In a final effort to prevent a complete deadlock, the Israelis made an extraordinary offer. They suggested that Jordan should be given a corridor one thousand metres wide, running from the Gulf of Aqaba, along and immediately adjacent to the Egyptian frontier, to the Gaza Strip. The corridor would be under the sovereignty of Jordan and would be demilitarised. In order to give the Israelis access to the port of Eilat on the gulf, there would have to be a crossing point near to the southern end of the corridor over which both parties would have the right of free passage. Obviously the idea offered no incentive to the Jordanians. Politically, it could not have been represented as the recovery of an important part of Palestine and, moreover, its acceptance would have started a wrangle between Jordan and Egypt over the ownership of the Gaza strip; administratively, it would have been a nightmare.

I was left wondering whether the offer was meant to be taken seriously. Be that as it may, it brought the talks to an end without their having done more than damage still further the King's reputation amongst his fellow

Arabs when the news of their occurrence leaked out. When I visited him in Tel Aviv months later Shiloah informed me that the talks had stretched his patience to breaking point.

I had been kept informed of the gist of the talks by the Prime Minister and I was neither disappointed nor surprised at their lack of concrete results. Once again, the two parties lacked the will or ability to make any acceptable concessions to the other side. It was a pity because the history of Palestine might have been different had they managed to come to an agreement. These exchanges, in so far as I was aware, were the last direct contact which the King had with the Israeli authorities although I am sure that means of communication were maintained.

In common with others who had attempted to rule the Holy City of three faiths, King Abdullah had found that the custodianship of the holy places of Christendom in Jerusalem and Bethlehem brought its own particular worries. The local representatives of the various Christian sects had been quarrelling with each other for centuries and they did not stop doing so because they were now at the centre of a war. His responsibility and the fact that he was party to the defiance of the terms of the United Nations resolution decreeing the internationalisation of the city, placed the King on the defensive and made him desperately anxious to avoid any action, or lack of action, which would lay the Jordanians open to the accusation of religious intolerance or of failure to safeguard the shrines of the three 'heavenly' faiths which had suffered relatively little damage during the fighting.

It was for these reasons, that the King was so perturbed when the main cupola of the Church of the Holy Sepulchre was found to be on fire one morning. The fire fighting services on the west bank were inadequate to deal with that type of conflagration and an official of the palace rang me up in a panic to ask if the fire fighting squad of the Royal Air Force station would be sent to Jerusalem to deal with the emergency. The orders in force at the time strictly forebad the entry of any service personnel into Palestine and there was not time to obtain permission from London for an exception to be made, so the Group Captain commanding at Amman and I decided to act on our own initiative and to send over a party of airmen dressed in civilian clothes. The men and their appliances were in action at the fire within a few hours and they extinguished the flames before they had done much damage. The inevitable rumour started that the fire had been lit by Jewish spies but, investigation proved the trouble to have been due to the carelessness of an Arab workman who was carrying out repairs to the roof with a blow lamp. A lingering spark had probably ignited the ancient timbers which were tinder dry.

There was another incident about this time which embarrassed me personally and which might have had serious political consequences if the affair had not been confined to exchanges in my study at my residence. It arose from a decision of the Iraqi government to retaliate for the expulsion of Arab refugees from Palestine by forcing the majority of the Jewish community of Iraq to go to Israel. Nuri Said the Prime Minister of Iraq, who was on a visit to Amman, came out with the astounding proposition that a convoy of Iraqi Jews should be brought over in army lorries escorted by armoured cars, taken to the Jordan-Israeli frontier and forced to cross the line. Quite apart from the certainty that the Israelis would not consent to receive the deportees in that manner, the passage of the Jews through Jordan would almost certainly have touched off serious trouble amongst the very disgruntled Arab refugees who were crowded into the country. Either the Iraqi Jews would have been massacred or their Iraqi guards would have had to shoot other Arabs to protect the lives of their charges.

The devious method employed by Nuri Said to make the suggestion was, in itself, enough to upset the King and the cabinet who still resented the way in which they had been left in the lurch by the Iraqi government in the armistice negotiations. Nuri first telephoned me asking to be received at my house with Samir Rifai to discuss an important question about Palestine. I agreed to the meeting on the natural assumption that Samir already knew all about it. Nuri then spoke to Samir and told him that I wanted to see both of them at my house. The latter assumed that the initiative came from myself. When we got together and Nuri made his proposal, and added the equally surprising statement that he would be responsible for the consequences, Samir and I were flabbergasted and our faces must have shown our feelings. Both of us were vexed at having been tricked into a false position.

I replied, at once, that the matter at issue was no concern of His Majesty's Government. Samir refused his assent as politely as possible but Nuri lost his temper at being rebuffed and he said: 'So, you do not want to do it, do you?' Samir snapped back, 'Of course I do not want to be party to such a crime.' Nuri thereupon exploded with rage and I began to wonder what the head of the diplomatic mission would do if two Prime Ministers came to blows in his study. We then broke up in disorder, but I got them both out of the house whilst preserving a minimum of propriety.

When I explained what had happened to King Abdullah, I asked him out of curiosity, what I should have done, according to Arab custom, if my two visitors had struck at each other. He answered: 'You could do nothing. As host you had to be strictly neutral between your guests and the only way for you to do that must be to stand back and let them sort out their differences as best they can.'

My embarrassment stemmed from the fact that Nuri Said had commanded the brigade of the Arab Army to which I had been attached during the year 1918 and had shown me great kindness. I still felt myself to be in his debt.

The next eminent visitor to come to Jordan was Prince Philip, the Duke of Edinburgh, who was a much more welcome personality to all of us. He arrived at Aqaba in command of a frigate, H.M.S. Magpie, on a purely naval occasion but, being who he was, a formal call on King Abdullah at Amman was indicated. I flew down to the port to meet the Duke and I brought him back to stay at my residence for a couple of nights. There was never any difficulty in keeping the conversation going between King Abdullah and members of the British royal family, their mutual interest in horses and guns always provided a topic. The dinner given in the Duke's honour was no exception but the talk came round to Jerusalem and Prince Philip expressed his desire to see something of the holy places. The King beamed and said: 'Go there tomorrow. I will see that all necessary arrangements are made for you.' This put me in a quandary because I could hardly say that the order barring service personnel from entering Palestine applied to the Duke also. It was sure that his involvement in an incident during an unauthorised visit would be most serious for both of us. I decided, however, to take a chance and raised no objection.

We went off early the next morning, stopping at the Allenby Bridge to fill with muddy water from the River Jordan an empty gin bottle, the only container which was available on the spur of the moment. The Duke told me, some years later, that the water was produced, still in the gin bottle, to be used at the christening of Princess Anne. Our first stop in Jerusalem was at the Garden of Gethsemane where were welcomed by a group of Greek Orthodox clergy who were delighted to receive a prince who had been brought up as a member of their church. Then we went on to the Church of the Holy Sepulchre before proceeding through the bazaars on foot to the Haram es-Sherif, where we saw the Dome of the Rock and the mosque of el Aqsa. Finally, we stood on the battlements of the citadel and looked across no-man's-land into Israeli territory. We were guests for lunch at the

Arab Legion command post on the heights of Mount Scopus. The Foreign Office received my report on the expedition with a silence which did not necessarily indicate approval.

The King delegated his eldest son, Talal, to go to Aqaba and return Prince Philip's call. I was pleased to see that Talal carried out his task with dignity. It was evident that the two princes got on well together.

Once my parish had been stretched to cover the west bank, still excluding Jerusalem, I made periodical visits to the district of Nablus and Hebron and resumed contact with the inhabitants there. There was little I could say, however, to cheer up the many persons who came to me in search of comfort about the future. I was moved by some of the older men who remembered the happier days of cooperation with the British and I recollect one of them saying to me in sorrow and reproach: 'I know that we did not always behave well towards you British, but have you not punished us enough?' Some of the younger and more politically minded men irritated me by putting all the blame for what had happened on the shoulders of the unfortunate British, while being void of ideas as to how they could remedy the parlous state of the affairs of their country.

The security controls on the Arab side of the armistice line were incredibly lax once one got off the main roads. One day, out of sheer curiosity, I drove down in my car to the point where the line crossed a secondary road in Samaria and the only indication that I had reached Israel was a small pile of stones in the middle of the track. There was no one in sight at first but, eventually, an affable young Arab villager, carrying a British service rifle, came up and wished me a good morning. I introduced myself and he accepted my *bona fides* without hesitation. He said that he was a watchman appointed by his fellows in the village to guard the boundary. When I asked him what he would do if a party of Israelis appeared suddenly before us, he answered that he would run away and give the alarm. He added that there had been no trouble in the neighbourhood so far.

In the course of these visits, I became interested in an Arab school for the blind which was operated as a private institution at Ramallah. Of the three hundred odd occupants of the building, only three persons were not blind to some degree or other. These were the wife of the director and his two children; the director himself had never seen. When walking about the place, I found it difficult to realise that the others could not see me and I felt, sometimes, as though I was living in a story by Edgar Allan Poe.

On my first call at the school, I found the local version of red tape trying to move the inmates out in order to use their quarters as government offices. The director appealed to me for help and pointed out that the staff and the children would be utterly lost in a strange place. It was no use my talking to the local officials about humanitarian considerations, so I went straight to the King. It was the sort of case with which he liked to deal and he stopped the move once and for all. He always fancied himself in the role of the benevolent father to his people.

CHAPTER 10

Talal

Few families, royal or otherwise, are without their problems concerning the personal relationships among their members. The Jordanian branch of the Hashemites was plagued by the chronic friction which existed between King Abdullah and his eldest son, the Amir Talal. Talal's mother, the daughter of the Sherif Nasser ibn Ali, was also a Hashemite and the first cousin of her husband. I have often wondered whether the trouble between father and son may have arisen because they were too much like each other. The fact remained that they never got on well together and that their relations worsened with time.

Whether or not Talal was born with the seeds of the mental illness which ultimately brought about his confinement to a hospital, is difficult to say, but it is certain that the state of constant rebellion against his parent aggravated the disease when it developed.

Talal was intelligent and when he chose to do so he could exercise the charm for which his family was remarkable. He was an affectionate and devoted husband and father after his marriage to the Amira Zein bint Jamil, his first cousin on his mother's side. She was a lady of great courage and character who fully reciprocated the attachment which her husband normally demonstrated towards her and their children.

Talal seemed to have an inborn dislike of anything connected with war and wore as infrequently as was possible the uniform of an officer of the Arab Legion, to which he was entitled. In spite of this, my predecessor, Sir Henry Cox, made the mistake, when he was British Resident, of combining with the King in compelling a reluctant Talal to become cadet at the Military Academy at Sandhurst. The experiment was disastrous and Talal's rebellious mood brought him into collision with both his teachers and his fellow cadets. He came home to Amman, more or less in disgrace, after the latter had thrown him into the pond in the college grounds.

Talal did not attempt to conceal his resentment at what had happened and his attitude, coupled with his notoriously bad relationship with the King, gave impetus to the widely spread existing rumour that he was anti-British. Throughout the Arab world it was reasoned that, if he disagreed with his father, who was a friend of the British, the prince must be against Great Britain. In point of fact, Talal did not differ from his father in regard to the policy which should be followed in relations with His Majesty's Government. The prince had many friends amongst the members of the British community in Jordan, in particular, Gerald Harding.

My wife and I had known Talal since he was a little boy and we remained on cordial terms with him and his wife. We used to have meals at each other's houses, *en famille*, before it was usual for Moslem ladies to meet their husband's friends socially. I frequently accompanied Talal on shooting expeditions in the desert, with his son, the Amir Hussein, acting as an honorary beater. I resisted the temptation to go and tell the King that I could not afford to wait until his decease before I got to know his heir, but I said something on those lines to those who warned me. I never knew whether my remark was carried back to the King.

In spite of the failure of the term in Sandhurst, Cox persisted in his efforts and he was instrumental in persuading Talal to accept two periods of attachment to British infantry regiments stationed in Palestine. With the earlier débacle in the background, Talal did not want to serve with a British unit and, sensing his resentment, his hosts did not welcome his presence in their midst. There was no unpleasantness on these occasions but both attempts faded out.

From that time onwards, Talal's mild eccentricity seemed to become more acute. It was not that any spectacular change took place, but he did odd things. For instance, there was an episode when we were out shooting in the desert with Talal at the wheel of his large American car. We were running across a mud-flat near to the oasis of Azraq, when I drew his attention to the fact that there was a damp patch of ground near to our route. He did not say anything, but he quite deliberately drove the car into the soft area and sat and laughed when we became well and truly bogged down miles from help. One never knew what he would do next. The trouble was progressive, and, in time, he got to the stage when, periodically, his peculiar behaviour bordered on mental abnormality.

The intermittent nature of the attacks of instability, between which he was normal and lucid, resulted in those quarters where Talal was believed to be anti-British, circulating the allegation that there was nothing wrong with his mental health and that the reports to the contrary were put out by the British in an attempt to discredit their enemy. It was inevitable that this situation should result in personalities and organisations which were inimical to the King and to Great Britain, attempting to use Talal as a focus for their activities in Jordan. It was to Talal's credit that those who made advances to him in such connections, got nothing but snubs for their pains.

During the early years of the Second World War, Talal infuriated his father by announcing that the Germans were winning the war. The King complained to me and described his son as a traitor. I made soothing noises and did not voice the opinion that many British people had come to the same conclusion about the course of the conflict.

After much hesitation, the King agreed to Talal being put under the care of Dr Ford Robertson who was the Principal of a large mental hospital in the Lebanon. The Amir actually resided at the hospital for a time, after which he was declared to be better and discharged. I heard stories of his having threatened to commit suicide whilst in the Lebanon and I was not convinced that Talal had been cured.

My doubts proved to be justified before very long. King Abdullah went on a state visit to Turkey in the spring of 1951, and Talal was appointed to act as Regent for his father. On the day of His Majesty's departure, we had all been to the airport at Amman to see him off, after which, I was settling down in my office to do some useful work. I had hardly got started when the palace telephone exchange operator rang through and asked me to speak to the Regent. When Talal came on to the line, he said: 'Good morning Excellency, can you please tell me where my father is?' When I recovered from my surprise, I replied, 'but your Highness, we all saw him off on an aircraft bound for Ankara, only about an hour's time back'. Talal came back with 'I know all about that but I think that my father has come back and is being hidden from me in the palace.' My enquiry, 'Had I better come and see your Highness at the palace?' was met with an abrupt 'No thank you. Do not bother.' I took him at his word and did nothing more.

Talal behaved rationally for about a week afterwards, then he rang me up again and asked if he could come and see me at my office. As his calling at my legation would give rise to gossip, I suggested that it might be best if I went informally to his house. He accepted my offer with alacrity and asked me to go there at once. He received me at the door of his dwelling with his accustomed courtesy, called for coffee and talked at random for so long that, ultimately, I asked him to come to the point. He said that the Amira had been taken to the Italian Hospital, where she was about to be delivered of a child, and had left him with the Armenian governess to look after the three boys. Would I be good enough to speak to the nurse who seemed to be upset about something? The girl in question was already known to my wife and myself so, after an initial refusal, I agreed to do what the Amir asked.

He ushered me into another room in which the nanny stood with his two younger sons, Mohammed and Hassan, then, without a word, he turned round and left the room closing the door behind him. I first asked the girl if everything was all right. She replied that it was but her unhappy expression belied her words. I then asked for news of the Amira Zein and, while we talked, I could hear a rustling noise coming from outside the door of the room. By this time, I was nettled with Talal's behaviour so I opened the door suddenly and practically caught him with his ear to the key hole. He was very taken aback and he saw me to the door in silence when I said: 'You must please excuse me. The nurse seems to be quite happy and I must do some work'.

When I got back home, I remarked to my wife that Talal appeared to be going mad. She rebuked me for being uncharitable and said that there was nothing the matter with Talal that a little kindness could not put right. She had never seen him during one of his bad phases and, like many others, refused to credit what was obvious. The King still affected to believe that Talal's queer conduct was an act which he put on to annoy.

The unfortunate truth became only too plain the next morning when my house boy awakened me about six o'clock and said that I had better get up because the Prime Minister had just walked into the house and demanded to be seen. I went down stairs to find Samir Rifai and Dr Jamil el Tutunji, the Minister of Public Health, waiting with long faces to tell me that Talal had threatened to murder his wife during the night.

Apparently, the Amira Zein had given birth to a baby girl in the course of the afternoon and had been visited by her husband afterwards. He had been perfectly normal during the first call, but she had awakened at three o'clock in the morning to find him standing by her bedside with a dagger in his hand. He had threatened her with the weapon and demanded to know who was the father of the child. I am sure that, if she had shown any signs of fear, he would have stabbed her, but, despite her alarm, she had had the nerve to pretend that she thought that he had been joking, He had dithered and while he did so, the ward sister, an Italian nun, who had been warned by the door porter that Talal had walked into the building, came in to the room to see what he wanted. When she realised what was happening, the sister, very pluckily, grappled with him and had wrested the dagger from his hand.

Having got possession of the knife, the sister had lost her head and had run across the corridor into another private ward which was occupied by an elderly Italian Archbishop, the Apostolic Delegate in Jerusalem, who was suffering from an attack of gout. I called on him the next day in order to find out for myself what had happened. He said, with a twinkle in his eyes: 'We priests see some funny things but I would never have believed that I would be awakened in the middle of the night by a nun running into my bedroom waving a bare knife in her hand'.

Talal took himself home and was left there with an aide-de-camp who was told to see that the Amir did not leave the house. I agreed with the Ministers that a message should be sent to the King asking him to cut short his visit to Turkey and to return to Amman. His Majesty arrived back in a state of considerable annoyance with those who had sent for him and he still refused to accept that his son was as unbalanced as we made out. He released the Amir from house arrest and expected everybody to behave as though nothing had happened.

Talal responded by making another attack on his wife and she issued an ultimatum to the effect that she and the children would no longer live in the same house as her husband. At this point, the King gave way and accepted the advice of the doctors that his heir should be sent to a mental hospital in Switzerland for treatment. It was thought best that the patient should be moved to somewhere outside the Arab world for the time being.

I did not see the Amir before he was sent away; I could not think what to say to him. He was still in Switzerland when I went on vacation leave to the United Kingdom in July 1951.

CHAPTER 11

Treachery

The strength of the military section of the Arab Legion was trebled from about seven thousand men to twenty-five thousand during the period of the fighting in Palestine and the performances of the Jordanian soldiers during that test gave them the well-deserved reputation of being amongst the best fighting material produced by the Arab race. The jealousy of some of the other Arab nations did not detract from the fame of the legionaries but rather tended to enhance it.

The value of the Arab Legion was, no doubt, appreciated by His Majesty's Government who were thinking in terms of building up a multilateral defence alliance in the Middle East which was to be called, later, the Baghdad Pact. It was clear that a friendly Jordan, with a strong army, could play a valuable role in such a grouping of countries. Nothing was said to the Arabs about such an alliance at that time, but a new readiness to provide more funds for a permanent expansion of the Arab Legion became apparent in London.

There was no shortage of candidates for enlistment to fill the enhanced cadre of the Legion but none of us realised how much the expansion would alter the nature of the force. The rapid increase in intake meant that the selection boards would be less exacting in the standards which they applied and that other factors would result in the enlistments including a greater proportion of men from the settled population. Prior to 1948, the Legion possessed no technical services and these were improvised during the hostilities with personnel who had studied in town schools and were, in consequence, politically minded. The new recruits also brought in an increasing number of Palestinians who felt no particular loyalty to Jordan or to the King. Lastly, the number of British officers was greatly increased, mainly by the appointment of personnel on secondment from the British armed services.

Both Glubb and I were uneasy about this last development but the War Office replied to our tactful suggestions that the overemphasis of the British element might lead to trouble in the future, by saying that it was their duty to ensure that the army for which they paid was efficiently trained and commanded and that, in their view, those two things could only be guaranteed by having British officers in the key posts. When I left Jordan at the end of 1951, on transfer to Libya, there were over sixty British officers attached to the Arab Legion, whereas there were only a handful of them when the corps made its name.

When the post war reorganisation had been completed, the bedouin units were as trustworthy as ever but there was less loyalty to the monarchy than before amongst the men of the formations which were recruited from the settled population. There were even reports current about a secret association of republican Free Officers whose members were plotting against the King and his British allies. These reports were not, alas, taken as seriously as they should have been by those in authority. It was a pity that Glubb had lost, by then, the intimate paternal touch with his men which had been of so great a value when the Legion had been a relatively small body. In other Arab countries there was a rising volume of jibes to the effect that it was odd to call a force which was commanded by British officers, a national Arab army. This was a damaging criticism which eventually put pressure on King Hussein to dismiss Glubb and his British colleagues in 1956. One realises, looking back, that the very success of the Legion undermined its dependability. One of the younger group of Arab officers who had come to the fore in the years 1948–49, was a certain Abdullah el Tel from Irbid, a town on the east bank. He had started his career as a customs officer and as such, he had managed to catch the eye of the King who had arranged for him to be given a commission in the Arab Legion. One of King Abdullah's faults had been favouritism which, as often as not, had been bestowed on unworthy persons. This was a case in point, and, until the final act of betrayal, preference was showered on Abdullah el Tel by his sovereign. He was promoted to Lieutenant Colonel when he was far from being a senior Major; he was frequently given special missions by the King in contacts with both the Arab and Jewish leaders in Palestine and, after the armistice agreement was concluded, he was appointed to one of the most senior posts in the civil administration that of Governor of Jerusalem.

Whilst holding that appointment, he called on Glubb and enquired as to whether he could be promoted to Brigadier if he left the governorship and resumed his duties with the Arab Legion. Glubb pointed out, in reply, that Tel had risen very rapidly from being a company commander eighteen months earlier, and, for that reason, it would not be possible to give him further advancement for the present. The two men appeared to part on amicable terms, but outward appearances proved to be deceptive.

A few months later, Abdullah el Tel resigned from the government service and went into sulky retirement in his native town in the north. Why he did so was never known with certainty but my guess is that the Egyptian Government must already have been tempting him to break his allegiance. He next moved to Cairo where the Ministry for Foreign Affairs gave him a furnished villa and an attaché in permanent attendance. The purpose of the move became evident when Tel embarked on a virulently hostile campaign over the Egyptian Broadcasting Service network and in the local press, aimed against the King, Glubb and myself.

As regards the King, Tel took the line that, as an Arab patriot, his conscience would no longer permit him to be party to the King's treacherous conduct towards the Arab nation and that he regretted having acted the part of intermediary with the Jews which the monarch had compelled him to play. These revelations about the King's contacts did not cause much surprise because the fact that they occurred was already widely known. One comment, which was frequently heard, was that it had taken a remarkably long time for Tel to discover that his role as messenger had been unpatriotic and that his dissent would have been more convincing had he resigned at the time. The Jordanians were perfectly well aware of Tel's indebtedness to the King's favour and they recognised and despised the base ingratitude of his betrayal.

The smears on Glubb and the other British officers of the Legion found a readier audience because there was already a tendency to treat them as scapegoats for the failure of the Arab armies on the field of battle. Tel made use of the call of the Free Officers for an Arab command of the national army as an effective weapon of propaganda against his former chief.

The principal theme of the attacks on myself was that as a foreign diplomatic envoy, I had no business to meddle to the extent which I did in the affairs of an independent kingdom. That line was out of date. It was true that I had interfered in the days when I had been the British Resident under the Colonial Office, and I had had every right to do so, but, since independence had come to the country, I had only proffered advice when it had been sought and the Jordanians had been perfectly free to disregard my views had they desired to do so. On the personal side, I had not known Abdullah el Tel well but I had never done him any harm. On the other hand, he had been on friendly terms with my eldest son when the latter had been an officer in the Legion during the Second World War. My son could never understand Tel's *volte face* but my explanation was simple. It was a case of too much pride; Tel had got on too rapidly to be able to keep his balance. He may have seen himself as a future Prime Minister.

The flood of abuse and accusations put out against the Jordanians by the Egyptian news media, was defeating its own object by its volume and repetitive content, so that Tel's contributions after his defection did not make any discernible impact as far as listeners in Jordan were concerned. Those who had been against the King remained hostile and those who had been his friends and supporters continued to be such. Something more than propaganda was brewing, however. The personal influence of the King amongst the east bankers was too deeply rooted to be destroyed by words and his enemies concluded that the only means of achieving their objective of reducing the Hashemite Kingdom of Jordan to a nonentity, or of destroying it, was to remove the man whose personality held the fabric of the state together. Thereafter, reports of plots against the King's life increased to an alarming degree and to my mind the atmosphere seemed to reek of murder and violence.

When I said goodbye to the King on the eve of my departure on vacation leave, I once again voiced my personal anxiety about his safety. He was in the habit of attending midday prayers on Fridays at el Aqsa mosque in the Haram es Sherif where an average attendance of several thousand worshippers made the effective screening of the congregation by the police an impossibility. I begged him, therefore, to pray at the mosque at Amman instead where he would be amidst his own people, but I came up against his fatalism once again. He smiled and repeated a poetic jingle in Arabic which meant, 'Until my day comes nobody can harm me: when my day comes nobody can guard me'. I could think of no answer to this piece of philosophy and I left him to find his fate.

My forebodings of death seemed to have been fulfilled when I read in the English papers of July 14th 1951, that Riadrh es Sulh, the Prime Minister of the Lebanon, had been shot and killed outside Amman whilst on an official visit to Jordan. Worse was to follow. Six days later, on July 20th which was a Friday, we were staying with an aunt of mine in the north and I went out after lunch for a walk with a cousin. My wife met us at the door on our return and, when I saw the expression on her face, it was obvious that there had been a disaster and my heart missed a beat as I thought of our sons. She beckoned me into the bedroom, gave me a telegram and said: 'It's Saidna, they have killed him. You are to go back to your post immediately'. I got through to the Foreign Office by telephone while my wife packed my clothes. They confirmed that the King had been shot dead at prayers in Jerusalem that morning. His day had come and the guard had been useless except to avenge his death.

Until I got settled down in a sleeping compartment on the train, I felt as though I was moving about in a dream, but as the full impact of the loss hit me I was filled with a great sadness. The fatal shot had brought to a close an association which had endured for over thirty years through weal and woe. During that period, the King and I had had our differences but, beneath the official relationship, there had been a deep personal friendship.

In London, I found that a passage had been reserved for me on a British Overseas Airways flight to Beirut which left that morning. The same aircraft was to carry the Amir Abdel Illah, the Regent of Iraq, who was the nephew of the late King, and a group of Iraqi politicians who were also bound for Amman. We were all to be picked up in Beirut by Arab Legion aircraft and flown to our destination. I did not feel like talking to anyone and, after a minimum exchange of condolences with the Regent, I spent the hours of the flight unhappily thinking

over the troubles which were likely to follow the disappearance of the father of his country.

My initial grief was replaced by a growing anger and
I resolved that if the King's murderers were arrested, there
should be no question of their being condemned for
periods of imprisonment and then amnestied, on some
pretext or other, as was done all too often in cases of
political killings in the Middle East. As a rule, I was
opposed to capital punishment, but I felt that my friend's
blood called out for vengeance.

There was an official reception organised by the
Lebanese Government at the Beirut airport for the Regent
and his party but I evaded an attempt to include me
in the function. I discovered that the second Arab Legion
Dove had been sent specially for me and I induced the
pilot to take off before the others had finished exchanging
compliments and drinking coffee. A large and tearful
crowd, headed by the Amir Naif and the cabinet, were
assembled at the Amman airport to meet the Iraqis and
I found their reception a moving occasion.

I was told the detailed story of the killing by the Prime
Minister. Apparently, there had been reports to the police
of an impending attempt on the King's life and despite
the frequency of such threats, more stringent precautions
than ever had been taken to protect him; so much so
that, just before entering the mosque, he had protested
to the commander of his guard, Habis el Mejali, that
he was being hemmed in by the soldiers. The assassin
had hidden between the wall of the mosque and one half
of the great door which had been flung wide open. The
leading guardsmen had not been able to see him as they
stepped across the threshold and they had given the signal
to advance into the building. When the King had paused
to allow the custodians to kiss his hand, the murderer
had leant forward, placed the pistol behind the King's
ear and had shot him through the head. When the King
had collapsed forward on his face, the guard had turned
inwards and had blasted the killer with bullets, his head

had been so badly shattered that it had been difficult to make out his identity. As was to be expected, the shower of bullets had wounded several of the guards and it had been little short of miraculous that the King's grandson, who is now the King of Jordan, who had been standing by the side of his grandfather, escaped unscathed.

The King died practically simultaneously in the arms of his personal imam, Sheikh el Shanqiti, who knelt beside his master on the blood stained carpets. I doubt whether he had seen the threat coming and I sought consolation in the memory that he had, on more than one occasion, expressed the wish to me that he should die suddenly some time before he became so old as to be a burden to his family.

In the absence of Talal in the sanitorium in Switzerland, Naif as the second son of the late King was the most eligible candidate for the post of Regent, though many people doubted whether he was really qualified to hold the post. A strong hand was needed at the helm because those of the Palestinian population who favoured the Mufti, were rejoicing openly at the ruler's death and there was a real danger of violent strife between them and the men of the east bank who were in a dangerous state of anger. There had already been clashes in the streets of Amman between the two factions and it was ominous that a Palestinian shopkeeper there had been shot dead by a policeman because he refused to close his shop as a sign of mourning when news of the assassination came through.

Samir Rifai and his colleagues were grateful for my moral support and, for the first time since 1948, I found myself restored to much the same position as that which I had occupied as British Resident when my advice was sought on most questions of importance.

The most immediate problem facing us was the interment of the late King. It was inevitable that feelings would run high at the ceremony and for that reason, the idea of a tomb in Jerusalem, near to that of his father, was rejected. The atmosphere in the Holy City was already explosive enough. A procession through the streets of Amman was also too risky and the most suitable alternative seemed to be a site somewhere in the grounds of the palace. That conclusion was agreed upon but the Ministers seemed to feel that it would be undignified if the body were simply carried over the one hundred and fifty yards from the main building to the spot chosen for the grave. It was, therefore, decided that the cortège should march in procession round the palace grounds and back.

Notable personalities, like foreign diplomatic envoys, were expected to say a ceremonious farewell to the deceased as he lay in state before the funeral. I put on formal clothes and went through the motions, but I can never feel much emotion over a dead body; it does not appear to me that there is anything there that matters of the dead person. The attendant officials probably expected me to make a scene but they were disappointed.

On the day of the burial service, most of the palace staff were in tears and their arrangements for the reception of the guests were chaotic. I had expected to feel mournful but, in fact, I was in a bad temper and my irritation was exacerbated by those who jostled with each other for precedence. The pious expression on the face of my Egyptian colleague, whose masters I believed to be responsible for the assassination, goaded me almost beyond endurance. As was fitting, the departed was given a soldier's funeral and the escort and firing party of the Arab Legion managed to get the cortège moving without too much delay. The troops in attendance were in a highly emotional state and I noticed a young bedouin private soldier standing with his rifle reversed and with the tears streaming down his face as we filed past to the slow beat of the drums.

The grave was dug in a field in front of the Royal Diwan and a tent was erected over the site pending the building of a permanent structure. When it was over, without

serious incident, I walked over to my house feeling empty
and exhausted. The most dramatic episode of the day
was the collapse of one of the firing party, after the prema-
ture discharge of his rifle, and his screaming imprecations
at the murderers and calls for vengeance.

General Robertson, the Commander-in-Chief of British
Forces in the Middle East, had come to Amman to attend
the ceremony. He had complained afterwards to Glubb
that I had neglected him. That may well have been so,
but I was in no mood to bother much about the civilities
normally extended to a very important person.

There was not much evidence to work on when the
police investigation got under way. The late King and
Glubb had received anonymous letters, threatening them
with death, a few days before the murder, but those were
not the first of their kind and there were no means of
identifying the writers nor of knowing whether there was
any connection between the letters and the deed. The
youth who fired the fatal shot was identified, with some
difficulty, as a tailor's apprentice who had no criminal
or political record. The British service revolver which fell
from his hand, gave no immediate clue as to who had
prompted the act.

The evidence given subsequently at the trial of those
arrested showed that the assassin had been assured of
a safe conduct to Egypt where he would have been treated
as a national hero, but the accused admitted that their
real intention had been to kill the young fool so that
he would not have been able to give evidence against
them had he survived the reactions of the guards.

The police officers in charge of the case were at a loss
for days, then an Arab woman went to a police station
in the Old City and stated that the revolver used by the
dead youth belonged to her husband who had been foolish
enough to announce that he intended to divorce her. The
denunciation was her revenge. Given a lead of so definite
a nature, the methods used by the Arab police could not
have failed to get at the truth before long. It transpired

that the owner of the weapon had lent it to the organisers of the crime knowing the purpose for which it had been intended. His testimony led to the implication of four men directly. The ring leader, who had borrowed the weapon, was a well known terrorist who claimed to have shot two Scottish soldiers in the back during the troubles of 1937–39. Another was Musa el Husseini, a cousin of the Mufti of Jerusalem and the other two persons were of no particular significance. The case of Musa was another instance of personal ingratitude; he and his father had been presented to the King at a private house in Jerusalem some years before and had, since then, always been treated with kindness by the monarch.

The four men in question must have realised that they were under suspicion but they made no attempt to escape and were arrested without difficulty. They denied their guilt but there was plenty of evidence against them when they were brought to trial. The trial was scrupulously fair, there was no need for it to be anything else, but I felt that their fate was sealed from the outset. There were people who would have made sure that they did not survive an acquittal for long.

Arrangements were made for members of the diplomatic corps to be admitted to the court without being submitted to the body searches inflicted on everybody else but I did not attend any of the proceedings and thereby caused some comment. Although I was prepared to exercise influence behind the scenes, I was anxious to avoid doing anything which looked like open interference.

The evidence indicated that the prime instigator of the plot had been Abdullah el Tel and he was tried *in absentia*. The trial was not lengthy and the four accused and Abdullah el Tel were condemned to death. Several others were placed on trial, including an Arab priest of the Latin Patriarchate in Jerusalem. The latter was known to have corresponded with Abdullah el Tel but the judges, luckily for the local Christian communities, decided that the priest had been nothing more than an ill-advised busybody. He and the remainder of the accused were acquitted. The four condemned men who were held in custody appealed against their convictions and had their applications dismissed. Abdullah el Tel ignored the court proceedings and the Jordanian government did not invite a rebuff by applying for his extradition. Few of us in Amman did not believe that the Egyptian authorities were the real culprits in the crime.

As I had anticipated, it was not long before pressure for the death sentences to be commuted to life imprisonment by the Regent was brought to bear by quarters both inside and outside Jordan. The idea behind the move being, undoubtedly, that, once the hangings were averted, it would only be a matter of time before the convicts were amnestied on some pretext or other. The Husseini clan were particularly active on behalf of Musa and, under their guidance, his attractive young German wife mounted a door to door campaign to save her husband's neck. She had the gall to come to my office and demand to see me on the subject, but I declined to receive her. I instructed my First Secretary, Christopher Pirie-Gordon to explain to her that the commutation of death sentences was no concern of the head of a foreign diplomatic mission.

Samir Rifai and the other Cabinet Ministers were firm enough in their resolve that the death sentences should be carried out and missed no suitable opportunity of strengthening their resolution. The Amir Naif, however, gave us trouble and he put off signing the warrants for execution on some pretext or other. He even went to the length of telling me that he saw no reason why he should incur unpopularity by sanctioning the hanging and that he proposed to let the matter wait until his brother, Talal, returned from abroad and took up the responsibilities of the heir to the throne. He enquired whether I thought that he was right and I retorted that it was not my father who had been killed. Even that unkind prod failed to move him to do his manifest duty.

Naif then made the mistake of going for a week's holiday to Lebanon, and left a Council of Regency in charge of the administration. Almost as soon as he was across the frontier, the members of the Council, who were all old supporters of the late King, signed the death warrants of the condemned. The executions took place a few days later. The terrorist who had borrowed the fatal revolver died badly and had to be dragged screaming for pity to the foot of the scaffold. Musa el Husseini babbled to the last moment about making a fresh start in South America. The remaining two men met their fate with quiet courage.

CHAPTER 12

The Succession

Logically, perhaps, the preceding chapter should have been the end of this story but, there is still something to tell before my personal tale of Jordan is complete.

Those who had hoped or expected that the internal situation in Jordan would suffer any immediate marked change for the worse, as a result of the loss of the late King, were disappointed. Samir Rifai, who was tired out with the strain, resigned shortly after the executions of the murderers of the King Abdullah, and he was replaced as Prime Minister by Tewfiq abul Huda once again. The small group of political leaders, which the late monarch had gathered round the throne, firmly held on to the reins of power, and while they were not friends amongst themselves, they had the wisdom to see that their failure to pull together could only bring harm to all concerned. As a result, the intrinsic stability of the regime enabled the country to ride out the stormy effects of a military defeat, the shock of the murder of the ruler and the intrigue over the succession to the throne which was to follow immediately.

The trouble over the succession stemmed from the dangerous practice, followed in some instances during the period of the mandate, of drafting an important law in English and then translating it into Arabic for enactment by the legislature. When dealing with two languages–structures of which differ so fundamentally, the possibilities of distorting the original meaning by the use of that method are readily apparent. In the case in point, the intention of the legislators was to apply the principle of primogeniture of the male descendants of the founder of the dynasty and that, indeed, is what the English version of the Organic Law provided for. However, the text of the Arabic version was not so clear and it was possible for it to be construed to mean that, if Talal did not succeed to the throne, the next member of the family in the line of succession would not be his eldest son, Hussein, but his half brother, Naif; the last named being the next oldest male of the descendants of King Abdullah. The difference between the two texts was due to an error in translation and not to a disagreement regarding policy.

The Head of the Royal Diwan at the time of the death of King Abdullah was a contentious and xenophobic gentleman, named Mohammed Shureiki, who, for some obscure reason, seized upon this discrepancy and argued that as Talal would never be mentally fit to ascend the throne, Naif should be proclaimed king without further ado.

The Amir Naif's background was largely Turkish. His mother was Turkish, he was married to a great-granddaughter of the Othmanli sultan of Turkey, Abdel Aziz, and he had been attached for a period of service with the Turkish army. He did not possess the typical charm and quick intellect of the Hashemite family. I was not in favour of Naif becoming king, not only because of my doubts about his capacity to be a successful monarch, but also because his accession would be attributed by many Arabs to a machiavellian plot on the part of the British Government to exclude their enemy Talal. Nothing could change the widespread belief that the reports about Talal's mental troubles were based on British lies.

Mohammed Shureiki managed to secure some degree of support for his contention from the opposition politicians and other troublemakers but the elder statesmen, headed by Ibrahim Hashem, Tewfiq abul Huda and Samir Rifai, shared my views. As regards Naif himself, he had never before shown any desire to interfere in the succession of the elder branch of the family but I suspected that his wife had ambitions, given an opportunity, to re-establish herself amongst the reigning royalty of the world once more. Be that as it may, Naif assumed the role of pretender to the throne of his father. He tried to win my support by inviting me to hunting parties in the desert but, after a couple of acceptances, I discovered that I was too busy to leave Amman.

Most of the responsible people in Jordan accepted the fact that Talal was not capable of dealing with the problems which were likely to arise in the near future and they wanted Hussein to succeed his grandfather and reign with a council of regency until he came of age. His Majesty's Government, who were not directly concerned with the problem, made it clear in their instruction to me that they were anxious that there should be no flaw in the legitimacy of the new monarch.

I discussed the question at length with the Prime Minister and we came to the conclusion that the best way of overcoming the difficulty created by the Arabic text of the constitution was for Talal to be brought back to Amman from Switzerland and placed upon the throne with the full realisation that he would probably not be able to reign for long. However, once Talal became king, there could be no further doubt about Hussein's right to follow his father as sovereign.

As this plan could only be put into effect with the support of the majority of the people, there could be no question of keeping it a secret. Once news of our intentions reached Naif's faction, the inevitable plots were set in motion to get Naif enthroned before his brother could be brought back home. Reports circulated from various quarters of plans to murder the young Amir Hussein but we did not take these too seriously. Nevertheless, he and his mother were given a permanent guard of bedouin troops as a precaution.

A more dangerous scheme then came to light; that of arresting all the ministers, after they had been summoned to the palace by the Regent, and their replacement by a newly appointed cabinet made up of Naif's supporters who would proclaim him King immediately. The danger arose from the fact that the palace was garrisoned by a sort of Pretorian Guard, called the Hashemite Regiment, which was recruited from the settled population and who were politically uncomfortably powerful. Mistakenly, this regiment had been allowed to acquire an exceptional extent of autonomy, so much so, that Glubb was not certain that its officers would obey his orders in preference to those of the Amir Naif if it came to a test of authority.

To counter this conspiracy, the Ministers agreed amongst themselves that no more than two of their number would go to the palace at one time. Two regiments of bedouin mechanised infantry were stationed at Amman, ostensibly for training purposes, but, it was no accident that the sites chosen for their camps dominated the palace and the main roads to and from the capital. It was intended that the building should be blockaded, or even stormed, if any of the Ministers were detained at the palace. I prayed, devotedly, that this contingency would never arise because my residence was close enough to the palace area to become involved if any fighting took place.

One of the most worrying factors in the situation was the possession by the Hashemite Regiment of an artillery section of six pounder anti-tank guns and some armoured cars. The use of these weapons would have made an assault on the palace a major operation. It was decided to try and prevent the situation developing into a stalemate by ordering the guns and the armour to be transferred to Mafraq for training exercises. If the order was obeyed, the Hashemite Regiment would no longer be a serious menace; if it was not obeyed, the nettle would have to be grasped. In the event the instruction was meekly carried out and the plot collapsed.

The way was now clear for Talal's return and proclamation as king. The day on which he returned, he was met at the airport by a strong detachment of armoured cars and, to make sure that there was no last minute hitch, he was driven straight to the parliament building where he took the oath of office and was invested as King before the assembled members of both the upper and the lower houses and the diplomatic corps of which I was doyen. There was, of course, no crown. The population in the streets showed so little enthusiasm for their new ruler that I felt the ceremony had taken on an air of unreality. In a sense, of course, it was all make-believe and I felt myself to be a fraud when I took the hand of the new King and wished him success in his work.

Many people were convinced that Naif had been the British candidate for the throne and I was amused to detect traces of commiseration in some remarks which were made to me after Talal's arrival. I did not try to correct the impression.

As soon as Talal's return became a certainty, Naif took umbrage and ceased carrying out his duties as Regent, but, he went to meet his brother at the airport, as protocol demanded, and he was present at the ceremony in the parliament. Talal was aware of what had been going on in his absence but both the brothers observed the necessary formalities in public. I do not know what they said to each other in private, but it was not an accident that before long, Naif moved to Beirut with his family, Mohammed Shureiki left his post in the Royal Diwan and the Hashemite Regiment was disbanded.

Superficially, all had appeared to be well after Talal took over but, one sensed that the authority of the monarchy had been undermined in spite of the fact that the public had shown little interest in the intrigue over the succession or in its outcome. Obviously the country missed the presence of the one man who was able to say, without fear of challenge, 'I know what is best for this kingdom because I built it up from nothing myself'.

The end of the series of crises should have left me relaxed and relieved but, instead, I was in a restless mood and suffered from an urgent desire to get away from Jordan for good. The disappearance of the man with whom I had worked for over thirty years left a bigger gap in my life than I realised at first. I got on well enough with King Talal and my wife was really fond of him and Queen Zein but, quite illogically, I resented seeing him sitting in his father's chair. I did not think that a holiday would cure my urge to move elsewhere so I wrote to Sir William Strang, who was the Head of the Foreign Service, and asked him whether there was anywhere else in the Arab world where my services could be of use. Strang offered me the appointment as first head of the British diplomatic mission about to be accredited to Libya once that country had been recognised as an independent sovereign state. I was very pleased about the idea of going to Libya as my brother had been Chief Administrator of Cyrenaica for the Military Administration and had managed to establish friendly relations with King Idris es Senussi. I accepted the post with alacrity.

I was committed to the transfer when I told the Jordanian Government of my impending departure and sought their agreement to my successor designate, Geoffrey Furlonge. Both King Talal and the Prime Minister asked me to change my mind and stay in Jordan, but I made out that the initiative had come from the Foreign Office and that the matter had gone too far to be reversed.

When the Israel Government heard of my transfer to Libya, they sent me an informal invitation to visit them in Tel Aviv. This was both a surprise and a compliment because, up to that time, they had refused entry visas to all British nationals, other than those of Jewish faith, who had been connected with the late Palestine Government. Once made, the visit could not have been concealed so I thought it best to consult Tewfiq abul Huda before accepting the offer. He looked surprised at the suggestion but he voiced no objections so I accepted.

I embarked on a series of farewell visits to various parts of Jordan and, some days before the date of the visit to Tel Aviv, I was in the Bahai village of Adessieh which was situated on the bank of the river Yarmuk where the frontiers of Jordan, Palestine and Syria meet. The debouchment of the Yarmuk gorge into the Jordan Valley was one of the more picturesque sights in a picturesque country. After lunch, for no particular reason, except to see the view, I took the village headman in my car and drove up the rough track on the Jordanian side of the ravine. While we stood at the viewpoint which was my goal, there was an outburst of firing on the other bank and we could see a certain amount of scurrying about of unidentifiable figures. Both my driver and the headman became nervous and the latter suggested that we should retire to the village immediately, otherwise someone would blame us for taking a part in whatever was going on. I stifled my curiosity and followed his advice.

I discovered that night from the local news, that we had witnessed the ambush by a party of Syrian troops, of two car loads of Israeli policemen from Tiberias who were patrolling the road to the sulphur baths of El Hammeh. All the policemen were injured and some of them were killed. In view of the tendency of people to misjudge one's motives, I felt that there were some grounds for the headman's fear of being blamed for involvement in the episode and I did not advertise the fact that I had been anywhere near the Yarmuk.

When I went to Tel Aviv, our Minister there, Knox Helm, sent his car to Jerusalem to collect me and I crossed the armistice line with a minimum of formality at the Mandelbaum Gate. I was given a pleasant surprise when the Israeli Governor of Jerusalem, Abraham Biran, met me at the frontier with a smiling welcome. As A. Bergman, he had been my District Officer at Afulah in 1937, when

I was District Commissioner of Galilee and Acre. I was touched by this personal attention on his part and on the part of his superiors.

The modern quarters of Jerusalem did not seem to have changed much under Israeli rule, but, once we had got clear of the suburbs and started to run downhill through the Judean mountains, I was struck at once by the luxuriant growth of the grasses and the other forms of wild vegetation. The explanation was that the Jewish economy did not include flocks of freely grazing goats whereas the land had been cropped bare by those destructive animals when it had belonged to the Arabs. Even in those early days, a great deal of agricultural development work was evident on every side, in marked contrast to conditions in Jordan.

As we debouched from the hill at Latrun, we passed near the Trappist monastery which had been my temporary refuge from the world for a few days during the Second World War. We also drove by a number of Jewish settlements which gave me the impression of being shabbier than those which I had known during the days of the mandate. When I mentioned this observation to some Israelis in Tel Aviv, they maintained that my recollection must have been at fault.

Helm very kindly put me up at his residence and took me the next day to pay a courtesy visit to the Israeli Ministry for Foreign Affairs. The office was still accommodated in the stuffy houses of the former German Templar colony of Sarona. The buildings were of a type which were more suited to the climate of northern Europe than to that of the Mediterranean coast. The Foreign Minister, Mr Sharrett, was out of the country and I was received by Mr Shiloah.

Shiloah and Helm steered the conversation to the future but I could not bring myself to contribute very much to the discussion. At heart, I was probably just as anxious as they were to see a settlement of the problem between the Arabs and the Jews and I had done my best on the other side of the river Jordan to secure peace but, now, I was going to North Africa and I did not want to be bothered any more about Palestine and its troubles. I sensed that both Helm and the Israelis felt that I was not justifying all the trouble which they had taken to arrange for my journey.

My host took me to a cocktail party that night where I was introduced casually to some people from the United States Embassy. One of the American attachés, who had evidently not gathered who I was or where I came from, made himself sociable by asking me whether I had ever crossed to the Arab side of the line. When I told him that I had just come over from my office in Amman, he looked startled and exclaimed, 'Amman, eh? But isn't that the enemy?' I nodded and he then hurried round the room to warn the others. The usual endeavours to extract useful information from me followed but they were a waste of time.

At the same party, General Yadin, the son of my archeological friend Mr Sukenik and then head of the Israeli General Staff, asked me if I had heard about the incident in the Yarmuk valley. He added that that afternoon, the nearby village of El Hammeh had been bombed from the air in reprisal for the ambush. I showed only a mild interest but enquired whether the bombing had been effective. Yadin described it as having been absolutely on target, but it appeared later on that the damage inflicted had not been serious and that the few Arab casualties had been people who could not possibly have had anything to do with the attack on the police.

The feeling that everybody was disappointed in my performance persisted the next day when I took my leave and started back for Amman. It was little consolation to realise that the Jews were suffering from the illusion, so popular and now so mistaken, that I was still all-powerful in Jordan and could make the King do anything I wanted. It was noticeable that no one turned out to see me back across the line at Jerusalem. Back in Amman, the trouble was, as it were, reversed and Tewfiq abul Huda expected me to tell him what the Israelis were up to. He hardly tried to conceal his disbelief when I told him that I had no news worth repeating.

The intention of the Foreign Office was that Blackley, the Chief Administrator of Tripolitania under the Military Administration should stay there as Minister for a few months until the newly independent state settled down. I was scheduled to move in and take over the post in about June 1952. Quite unexpectedly, the programme was upset by King Idris who declined to accept the appointment of Blackley on the grounds that it was not acceptable for a person to become a diplomat where he had exercised authority as a military governor immediately beforehand.

His Majesty's Government were determined that their representative in Libya should be the doyen of the diplomatic corps or, in other words, that he should be the first head of mission to present his letters of credence. Now that Blackley was no longer eligible, it meant that in order to qualify as doyen, I would have to arrive in Libya a few days before December 24th 1951, the date on which the declaration of independence would be made.

The deadline barely left me time enough to go to London for briefing before taking up my new post. I could not possibly have stayed at Amman long enough to close down my house so, once again, my wife would have to remain behind to pack and later to follow me.

Official and private leave taking after being at a post for a long spell is usually a lengthy process which includes numerous meals and cocktail parties but I had to cut the business short and confine myself to attending the formal dinner at the palace and another meal given in my honour by my colleagues in the diplomatic corps. In a sense, I was rather relieved that there was so little time because I found the breaking of the ties of a lifetime to be more painful than I had anticipated.

My anxiety to get away from Amman was magnified by the unpredictability of King Talal's reactions in any given circumstances. King Abdullah had had his faults as well as his virtues but those of us who had worked for him for decades were able to foresee what he was likely to decide and we had developed our own techniques for influencing him in the direction we wished to take. Now, we were dealing with a man who might do anything at any moment. In the event, King Talal realised that the burdens of office were too much for him and he abdicated willingly about five months after I had left Jordan.

The journey to London via Amsterdam and Damascus was a nightmare; everything seemed to go wrong. I left home in a mood of black depression and, as I was driven past the grave of my old friend, I felt that the end of that particular story had indeed been reached. It was raining when we left Amman and, once we were over the Syrian frontier, the downpour became so heavy that the river flooded across the main road at Kisweh and we were compelled to make a long detour which brought us to the legation at Damascus shortly after midnight instead of in time for dinner. The next morning, the KLM aircraft left for Amsterdam five hours late and lost more time as the journey proceeded, with the result that we reached Holland, via Athens and Nice, at three o'clock in the morning with all connections for London well and truly missed. A heavy cold in addition to my mental depression made me a sorry wreck when I finally reported to the Foreign Office.

When I left Amman, it was nearly thirty-four years since I had commenced my work in Jordan in February 1918. Most of that period had been spent in the relatively rewarding task of building up a national entity and an administration on the scant foundations which had been left by the Ottoman Turks when they withdrew. The time covered by these recollections passed in a struggle to preserve the structure created by King Abdullah and his supporters. Now, as I left the country for good, it looked superficially the same, but time was to show, that Jordan was poised on the top of a long slope down which it was to slide into the passionate bloodstained instability now characteristic of so much of the Arab world.

Note on Prime Ministers

Three of the Prime Ministers who held power during the formative years of the history of Jordan played outstanding parts in the administration of the affairs of the country. Although they competed for office amongst themselves and did not see eye to eye in some matters of policy, they were faithful supporters of King Abdullah and they implemented the main lines of his directives. Their principal value stemmed from the fact that they put the interests of the country before their personal disagreements and ambitions.

IBRAHIM HASHEM was born in Nablus in 1894 of land owning stock. He graduated in Turkish law and was conscripted into the ranks of the Turkish army during the First World War. He deserted in 1917 and remained in hiding until the British occupation of Palestine. He joined the administration of Jordan in 1921 and held various legal and ministerial posts until 1958 when he was killed by a mob in Baghdad during the Iraqi rebellion against the Hashemites. At the time of his death he was deputy Prime Minister of the brief and ill-starred union between Iraq and Jordan.

TEWFIQ ABUL HUDA was born in Acre about the year 1898 of a well-to-do family of the merchant class. He received his secondary education at Stamboul and he served as an administrative officer in the Turkish army during the First World War. He joined the civil administration in Damascus in 1918 but moved to Amman in 1922 where he specialised in finance and land registration. He served numerous terms as Prime Minister. He suffered from an incurable cancer and committed suicide in 1957.

SAMIR RIFAI was born in Safed about the year 1902 of a family who followed a tradition of becoming civil servants. He was educated at the Scot College at Safed and joined the Palestine Government in a clerical post. He next moved to Amman where he was employed for a time at the Royal Air Force camp before obtaining an appointment with the Jordanian administration. In later life he was active in the creation of the university of Amman. He died of heart failure in 1967.

Index